Foreword

Kay Kotan brings out the best in people and their churches. If you browse through the oeuvre of more than a dozen books Kay has written, you will notice that Kay rarely writes a book alone. As Jesus sent the disciples two-by-two, so Kay tends to write. Kay has the gift of identifying talent in the Church and magnifying the impact of that talent. In *Inside Out*, Kay has once again identified, connected with, and is magnifying the impact of a talented leader in Michael Scott to offer this resource for churches seeking to effectively adapt to the cultural changes taking place in our world.

I first met Kay as we represented our respective conferences at the 2016 South Central Jurisdictional Conference of The United Methodist Church (UMC). I was the pastor of La Fundición de Cristo (Christ's Foundry United Methodist Mission) in Dallas, Texas, the largest Spanish-language congregation in The UMC at the time. Kay is one of the leading experts in church vitality and has assisted thousands of congregations to live into their mission, and her reputation for insightful leadership preceded our meeting. As someone who always wants to learn from the best, I walked across the restaurant in a crowded restaurant full of United Methodists in Wichita, Kansas and introduced myself to Kay. There I had the first of many insightful conversations with Kay that have assisted me as a leader.

A year later, after meeting Kay, Bishop Michael McKee appointed me to my current appointment as the Director for the Center for Church Development of the North Texas Conference. In this position, I am charged with leading church planting, congregational vitalization, and strategic initiatives for the UMC in North Texas. Kay has held a similar position in three different conferences. Again, as someone who wants to learn from the best, I contacted Kay for advice and mentoring shortly after assuming this role. Her dedication to helping the Church once again was demonstrated in the generosity of her time and expertise that she extended to this rookie developer.

Today, I continue to keep Kay's number close. I have leveraged Kay's expertise in the North Texas Conference for training, coaching, and equipping clergy and laity on various projects. From helping churches improve their governance, to assisting congregations with pastoral transitions, to coaching individual pastors and projects, church work is made better by Kay Kotan.

In 2022, I hosted the national gathering of United Methodist church developers as well as a national gathering of UMC church planters. Obviously, I wanted Kay to present whatever Kay was currently working on. In preparation for this national gathering where Kay would present, she introduced me to Michael Scott.

Michael and I first met by Zoom in 2021, and I was immediately captivated by his story, vision, ministry, and, yes, his name (I am a fan of The Office). Michael is an effective church planter and is developing a sustainable church planting model that includes ministering to various affinity groups in creative ways on and outside of Sundays while diversifying the income streams of the congregation. Church planting (or growing a church) has never been more challenging in the United States of America as it is today.

As Kay has the gift of finding talent and magnifying the impact of that talent, on my first Zoom with Michael, I could see why Kay said to me, "You need to meet Michael Scott."

Glowing reviews were given for Michael and Kay's presentation at our national gathering. In their presentation, they introduced many concepts found in *Inside Out*. I have followed up with both Kay and Michael to help the North Texas Conference with some projects we are working on here, specifically on how to leverage early childhood education to disciple young children, minister to young families, and provide additional income for the church (in that order of priority). The knowledge and experience of Michael and Kay on leveraging ministry for mission and income are a gift to congregations that are struggling to reach their mission field and struggling to fund strong ministries.

Inside Out gives the reader not only an introduction to diversifying income streams but is designed primarily to equip and empower congregations in their mission. I have seen congregations that were able to diversify their income streams, only to have an alternative income stream to simply fund the hospice care of a dying congregation. The world needs more from the Church than the Church simply seeking to sustain itself.

In the 49th Chapter of Isaiah, God says to Isaiah it is too small a thing to restore just the congregation or to gather those who have left. The Church must be outward-focused and the light of the world we were created to be. *Inside Out* helps move the Church out of old templates and into the mission field. *Inside Out* not only inspires but also equips the Church to break out of the molds that hold back our light from shining its brightest.

Finally, if possible, I recommend that you do not read this book alone. *Inside Out* is an interactive instrument "to equip the saints for the work of ministry, for building up the body of Christ" (Ephesians 4:12 NRSVUE). I encourage you to find colleagues or others in your congregation with whom you can study and implement this book in community. The Church needs this book now. I am confident your church can use this book now. Shifts are happening in the religious landscape, and churches will either adapt or become irrelevant. Irrelevancy is not an option for the Church today. Therefore, I am honored and eager to commend *Inside Out* to you. Get ready to evert your church!

Owen K Ross, DMin
Director, Center for Church Development
North Texas Conference of The United Methodist Church

inside
OUT

Everting Ministry Models
for the Postmodern Culture

Kay L. Kotan & Michael J. Scott

Foreword by Rev. Owen Ross

Market
Square
BOOKS

Inside Out

Everting Ministry Models for the Postmodern Culture

by Kay L. Kotan & Michael J. Scott
Foreword by Owen Ross

©2022 Market Square Publishing, LLC

books@marketsquarebooks.com

141 N. Martinwood Dr., Knoxville TN 37923

ISBN: 978-1-950899-64-7

Printed and Bound in the United States of America
Cover Illustration & Book Design ©2022 Market Square Publishing, LLC

Editor: Sheri Carder Hood
Post-Production Editor: Ken Rochelle

Scripture quotations used with permission from:

CEB
Scripture quotations from the COMMON ENGLISH BIBLE. © Copyright 2011 COMMON
ENGLISH BIBLE. All rights reserved. Used by permission. (www.CommonEnglishBible.com).

MSG
Scripture quotations marked MSG are taken from THE MESSAGE,
copyright © 1993, 2002, 2018 by Eugene H. Peterson. Used by permission of NavPress,
represented by Tyndale House Publishers. All rights reserved.

NRSV
New Revised Standard Version Bible, copyright © 1989 National Council
of the Churches of Christ in the United States of America.
Used by permission. All rights reserved worldwide.

NRSVue
New Revised Standard Version Bible, copyright 1989,
Division of Christian Education of the National Council of the Churches of Christ
in the United States of America. Used by permission. All rights reserved.

The Voice
Scripture taken from The Voice™. Copyright © 2012 by Ecclesia Bible Society.
Used by permission. All rights reserved.

Table of Contents

Introduction

Here's the church.
Here's the steeple.
Open the door.
See all the people.

Like us, you probably learned this rhyme along with the hand motions growing up in children's Sunday school. Take a moment and reflect on those words and the associated hand motions likely steeped in English history.

There are three key observations we would offer for your consideration. First, "the church" refers to the building. Second, the idea behind the rhyme is that "all the people" are already gathered in the church under the steeple since we must "open the door" to "see all the people." Third, when using the hand motions, we invert our hands in order to see the people.

Let's unpack these three observations and how they are steeped in our church-centric understanding of a culture we know no longer exists. Unfortunately, many churches still operate as though the church-centric culture does indeed still exist.

Observation One

- As a child, we were taught that the church was the building. While we intellectually understand that the church is the people, a congregation often makes decisions that lead us to believe that perhaps this is not the case.

Observation Two

- This innocent rhyme taught the attractional model of church: People will gather if you just open the church doors.
- All you have to do is open the door to see all the people.

Observation Three

- When we were taught as a child to twist our wrists so that we no longer had to peer through the door (our thumbs) to see all the people, the seed was planted for the eversion lesson we must now learn for the postmodern world we now find ourselves living in.

As we evert the church model for the postmodern, post-Christian world, we need to evert—turn inside out—many of our thoughts and beliefs about how we go about "doing" church. This is NOT about changing our beliefs but about changing how we engage in ministry. Jon Ritner[1] suggests we must "exchange the mission from creating

---

[1] Positively Irritating: Embracing a Post-Christian World to Form a More Faithful and Innovative Church, page 155.

a community to becoming a community that pursues God's mission." Ritner explains, "When you lead with community you rarely get a group that engages in the mission, but when you lead with mission, deep community is formed as a byproduct."

As our faithful first step in this hard-but-holy work, we must evert our thinking to enable us to evert our actions and ultimately increase the Kingdom's impact. In working with pastors and church leaders for more than a dozen years, I (Kay) often witness how the thoughts, ideas, and strategies of the most faithful automatically revert to old ways of thinking and doing church. Even those who consider themselves innovative and outwardly focused often find themselves stuck in rutted thinking and doing without even realizing it. We need a HUGE, SEISMIC paradigm shift to break this unrecognizable barrier.

There is a growing gap between the churched and unchurched population in America. In 2021, the scales tipped. For the first time in history, more people reported that they are NOT affiliated with any church than those who are affiliated with a church. Less than half the population report religion being important to them. Yet there is a growing population especially amongst those under age 40 who report being spiritual, but not religious. This means us church-going Christians are now the minority. Despite these findings, we Christians often continue to act as though we are still the majority of the population by what we desire and expect of people in our communities and country. When the church can come to this realization, we will begin to wrap our heads around the need to think about being a spiritual community in a different way. Until the church recognizes and accepts this foundational shift, we will continue to struggle as a church and ultimately struggle to narrow the gap between the churched and unchurched. We must begin to acknowledge this new reality and approach building our spiritual community in a different way.

Please join us on this journey—this treacherous, holy journey. Throughout this resource we are indeed encouraging you to turn your faith community inside out. You may feel like you are being twisted, stretched, pushed, pulled, and literally turned inside out. We understand. It's okay. Thank you for being bold and courageous enough to trust us as your journey partners. We invite and challenge you to evert your ministry starting today.

It is time to evert the ministry model!

*Evert from Sunday-Centric to
Relationally Focused*

*Evert from Building-Centric to
Community Minded*

*Evert from Pastor-Centric to
Laity-Driven*

*Evert from Offering Plate Dependent to
Multiple Streams of Income where mission is accomplished*

It is time to turn ourselves INSIDE OUT!

*From INSIDER-focused to an
OUTSIDE deployed movement*

*From INSIDER-preference-driven to
OUTSIDE focus on the community*

*From INSIDER asset consumption to
OUTSIDE people investment*

*From INSIDER care to
OUTSIDE transformation of the community*

*From INSIDER education to
OUTSIDER focus with the Holy Spirit's
transformation of us and our neighbors*

There is urgent kingdom work that needs to be done. The postmodern, post-Christian world is suffering. People are more connected digitally than any prior generation but find themselves lonelier than ever before. Our neighbors seek hope, meaning, and a sense of community and belonging. Mental health is in crisis with staggering levels of depression and anxiety. While our neighbors struggle and need help, so many churches are ill-equipped for this work—the kind of work the church should be the very best at providing. After all, we have the Good News. Sadly, though, our methods of sharing this Good News and reaching others outside our congregations are no longer relevant, so it is as though the church is mute and the community culture is deaf or vice versa.

What we will unpack in this resource are the emerging church trends in our American culture. If the church is to be relevant, compelling, and faithful in its commission to reach new people, we must embrace these trends and plot a new course to navigate them in our local contexts. The need for this navigation and course correction is critical, and the timing is urgent. We have no time to waste. The church has remained hesitant for too long as culture has charged forward by leaps and bounds. There is no more waiting. The time is now. The mission is too important to delay any longer.

How to Use this Resource

This book is written as a resource for leaders and groups to work through together. Some of the statements and suggestions within these pages will likely be challenging. We certainly understand. Yet, that's exactly why we felt called to create this resource. It is intended to name the needed shifts, help you begin conversations in your church, and provide some possible first steps.

Undergird the reading, processing, discussing, and ultimately the implementing of this resource with prayer. This is sure to be hard-but-holy work. We suggest the church leaders and participants study this book together. Take one chapter at a time (i.e., weekly or monthly). Everyone should read and reflect privately on each chapter, journaling their thoughts on the Story, Evaluation, and Questions at the end of each chapter.

Once the group comes together, use these steps to make the most of this resource:

- **Open with prayer**, asking God for all gathered to remain open to the Holy Spirit's movement, God's preferred future for the church, and for us as leaders to not stand in the way of anything God desires.

- **Cover the key points** of the chapter. Ask each person to identify key points from the chapter.

- **Process the Evaluation together** by first sharing individual scores and why particular leaders scored as they did. Sharing this will provide helpful insights for one another. Next, identify the Evaluator score that the overall leadership team lands on for the topic. Cover each of the ten topics under the Evaluator using this same process.

- **Discuss the five questions at the end of the chapter**. Ask each leader to share their answer to the question. Having each leader share their answers provides fuller insights and alternative views.

- **Before dismissing the leaders**, identify any faithful next steps to be taken. Is there any information/data to be collected? Is there any communication that should be shared with the congregation?

- **Pray together** once again and continue to keep one another in prayer throughout the journey together through this resource to discern how God will work through it and you for God's purposes.

We thank you for being bold, courageous, and open to journey through this resource with your leaders. May it be a blessing to you personally, to your faith community, to your community, and ultimately to the individuals who will come to know Jesus because you took this determined, faithful step.

CHAPTER ONE
Moving Away from Sunday-Centric

*Even though I am free of the demands and expectations
of everyone, I have voluntarily become a servant to
any and all in order to reach a wide range of people:
religious, nonreligious, meticulous moralists, loose-living
immoralists, the defeated, the demoralized—whoever.
I didn't take on their way of life. I kept my bearings in
Christ—but I entered their world and tried to experience
things from their point of view. I've become just about every
sort of servant there is in my attempts to lead those I meet
into a God-saved life. I did all this because of the Message.
I didn't just want to talk about it; I wanted to be in on it!*

I Corinthians 9:19-23, MSG

There was once a time when our culture literally
stopped on Sunday. No stores, restaurants, or gas
stations were open for business. People stopped and
rested. Life deliberately slowed on Sundays to celebrate
the sabbath. Society was mostly Christian, and the
church was the center of the community. People felt
a sense of obligation and responsibility to attend
church. After church, extended families often flocked
to Grandma's house to spend extended time together,
gathered around the table for a meal.

The "blue laws" (aka Sunday law) that prohibited businesses from being open on Sundays date back to 321 AD:

Industrialization mostly destroyed this system, but some pieces of it, like abstention from work during churchgoing hours in Christian societies, either remained normative or were enshrined in law. In the United States, "blue laws," named for the blue paper on which Puritan leaders printed the Sunday trade restrictions, date back to the 18th century at least. Many forms of commerce were regulated or restricted so that workers should spend time in church or with their families.[2]

But as more and more states began to repeal the blue laws, starting in the 1960s, the US population has identified itself less and less as Christian. In court cases defending the blue laws, their purpose was cited by Chief Justice Earl Warren[3] in 1961 as "the State seeks to set one day apart from all others as a day of rest, repose, recreation and tranquility—a day which all members of the family and community have the opportunity to spend and enjoy together, a day on which there exists relative quiet and disassociation from the everyday intensity of commercial activities, a day on which people may visit friends and relatives who are not available during working days."

In a Supreme Court case in the same year, the blue laws' purpose was cited as, "while such laws originated

---

[2] https://www.vox.com/the-big-idea/2018/10/2/17925828/what-were-blue-laws-labor-unions.

[3] https://en.wikipedia.org/wiki/Blue_law.

to encourage attendance at Christian churches, the contemporary Maryland laws were intended to serve 'to provide a uniform day of rest for all citizens' on a secular basis and to promote the secular values of 'health, safety, recreation, and general well-being' through a common day of rest. That this day coincides with Christian Sabbath is not a bar to the state's secular goals; it neither reduces its effectiveness for secular purposes nor prevents adherents of other religions from observing their own holy days."[4]

While more and more options opened up for people to enjoy on the weekends, one can point to a direct correlation to the decline in church worship attendance. While there is an obvious connection, this societal change is not the only reason for the decline. A few other reasons include the following:

- We have erroneously linked the sabbath and going to church on Sunday as one and the same. Sabbath is about rest and renewal.

- The church became insular and forgot its purpose of reaching new people. It is the only organization that does not exist for the benefit of its members.

- Discipleship morphed into Christian education. The furthest distance is from the head to the heart. Without transformation, Christian education is hollow.

---

4 https://en.wikipedia.org/wiki/Blue_law.

- The church shifted to emphasize membership and benefits without expectations, accountability, and responsibilities.

- As more women entered the workforce, there were fewer servant leaders to carry out the ministries of the church.

- Because of the churches' insular focus, churches grew ever more culturally incompetent and irrelevant, making it increasingly difficult to reach the unchurched.

- Society shifted towards a distrust of institutions and institutional leaders.

- Because of technology, greater knowledge and proof of religious leaders' indiscretions were more easily detected and reported, adding to the distrust of religious leaders.

- Secular youth and children's activities are now more likely than ever before to be scheduled on the weekends. Current churchgoers often cite that families have their priorities and values out of whack, but we think churches may need to reevaluate their children and youth ministries. Much of what our churches offer children and youth today is no longer relevant or compelling, leaving them without the opportunity to experience a community outside their family and school—their "third place." Because of this lack of offerings in the church, parents have sought activities elsewhere. The ball fields, dance studios, and recital halls have become these children's and youth's "third places." What if the church was the place to provide these opportunities? More on that later in this book.

Options and Convenience

We live in a 24/7/365 world. The world never sleeps and never stops. Even during the pandemic, people adapted, worked, and schooled from home to keep the world spinning on its axis. It is now commonplace to have groceries, meals, clothing, and other essentials delivered to your door rather than shopping in person. With the touch of a button, one can order almost anything from toothpaste to caskets online and have it delivered straight to them. We now possess a deeper understanding of our interconnectedness as the pandemic revealed how interdependent countries have become on one another. Supply-chain disruptions in one country shut down assembly lines in other countries.

While Americans already took advantage of the many life conveniences, the pandemic served up another helping of convenience out of necessity. One of those conveniences was the option of more online worship experiences. Rather than getting the children out of bed, dressed, fed, and out the door to attend an in-person experience, the family now had the option to enjoy a leisurely Sunday morning at home, eating their pancakes and joining worship online in their jammies.

Beyond the option of live-streaming versus on-site worship, there was—and still is—the option of viewing a recorded version of worship later in the week or month that might better fit one's schedule. The number of views for a church's online worship often doubles—or more—after Sunday. Let's face it, people like options and flexibility. Not everyone is off work on Sundays. Some families have activities scheduled on Sundays. Younger generations appreciate experiences more than possessions; therefore, more frequent and extended travel is part of their normal life rhythms. Extended families do not always live nearby, so weekends are often used to travel to see grandparents, sisters, brothers, cousins, aunts, uncles, etc. Many families are blended. Children spend some weekends with one parent and another weekend with the other parent. This means that both children and parents have different routines and availability for those weekends. Even the Boomer generation's attendance patterns have declined in the past several years as they travel for leisure and visit grandchildren out of town.

Take a moment and reflect on the Acts scripture below. These scriptures describe the primitive church when it was at its youngest, most innocent, and most faithful in following spiritual practices. As a result, their ministry impact was multiplying daily.

The community continually committed themselves to learning what the apostles taught them, gathering for fellowship, breaking bread, and praying. Everyone felt a sense of awe because the apostles were doing many signs and wonders among them.

There was an intense sense of togetherness among all who believed; they shared all their material possessions in trust.

They sold any possessions and goods that did not benefit the community and used the money to help everyone in need.

They were unified as they worshiped at the temple day after day.

In homes, they broke bread and shared meals with glad and generous hearts.

The new disciples praised God, and they enjoyed the goodwill of all the people of the city. Day after day the Lord added to their number everyone who was experiencing liberation.

Acts 2:42-47 (VOICE)

Now reflect on this same scripture paraphrased by Kevin Slimp, author and publisher, for his Sunday school class on July 10, 2022. His paraphrase offers a succinct insight into the shifts we have been noting. He titled it, *Kevin's Modern Paraphrase of Acts 2:42-47 for Today's Church:*[5]

The Fellowship of the Believers

They devoted themselves to the most popular online TV preachers, to Christian radio, and to prayer. Everyone was filled with awe at the guitar licks, stained-glass windows, and enormous structures. All the believers were together for one hour each week, unless it was a holiday or a really nice day outside. Some met together to distribute food to the needy every few weeks. Now and then, some of them would meet together at a restaurant, but rarely entered each other's homes.

And the number of believers decreased steadily each year.

---

[5] Kevin Slimp, *Kevin's Modern Paraphrase of Act 2:42-47 for Today's Church,* Open Door Class, Middlebrook Pike United Methodist Church, Knoxville, TN.

Shifting Priorities

The pandemic ushered in yet another shift in our culture: a change in priorities. Along with the drastic overnight changes in people's rhythms and routines came the opportunity for people to reflect on what was truly important to them and what they ultimately valued. The pandemic forced people to stop and reflect. This reflection disrupted the labor force, which we now know as the "Great Resignation" or the "Great Reshuffling."

Beginning in April 2021, the Great Resignation started when a record number of workers, 3.8 million people, quit their jobs. In the following months, those numbers continued to increase:[6]

> May 2021. . . . . 3.6 million
>
> June 2021 . . . . 3.87 million
>
> July 2021. . . . . 4.03 million
>
> August 2021 . . . . 4.27 million
>
> September 2021 . . . . 4.43 million

According to the Bureau of Labor Statistics, an estimated 47.8 million people quit their jobs in 2021. Some of the top reasons cited by millennials were that they value purpose over a paycheck, they want skill development, and they desire a coach rather than a

---

[6] https://www.yahoo.com/video/number-americans-quitting-jobs-2021-160334757.html.

boss.[7] "After discovering that nearly half of America's workforce is job searching or keeping an eye out for new opportunities, researchers from Gallup concluded that "the great resignation is really the great discontent." Rather than being an issue with pay or industry, the researchers said: "The pandemic changed the way people work and how they view work," according to Forbes. Gen Z workers desire jobs that allow them to pursue their passions and purpose. They don't want anything to do with busy work or strict 9-5 schedules.[8]

As culture has shifted and the rhythms of people's lives have changed, how effective is the Sunday morning experience in living out the mission of the church? In Jon Ritner's book, *Positively Irritating*,[9] he offers this insight: "It felt like the impact only reached as far as people's interlexical beliefs and religious habits. What we did on Sunday didn't seem to carry over to the other six days of the week."

Now the tough question we must wrestle with is this: If the Sunday morning experience is not growing and transforming the existing congregation, nor is it reaching new people, is there a more effective way to reach people? What would a less Sunday-centric approach look like?

[7] https://www.michaelpage.com/advice/management-advice/development-and-retention/5-things-millennials-look-job.

[8] https://www.forbes.com/sites/jasonwingard/2021/09/02/the-great-resignation-why-gen-z-is-leaving-the-workforce-in-drovesand-what-to-do-about-it/?sh=19a3cd825f87.

[9] https://www.amazon.com/Positively-Irritating-Embracing-Post-Christian-Innovative/dp/1735598801.

Rethinking Sunday

During a presentation in Kansas City in October 2021, David Kinnamon, President of Barna Group, made a direct correlation between the 2009 movie *He's Just Not That into You* and the post-pandemic church. He explained that many churchgoers were just not that committed to the church. Once the pandemic interrupted their participation and attendance patterns, they easily fell into new patterns. The once "Sunday church-attenders" now enjoyed more flexibility in their weekend schedules for travel, sleeping in, new hobbies, enjoying nature, and more. Maybe they just weren't as into the church as we thought. Or maybe they found a new way to explore their spiritual life that is a better fit or is maybe an even more meaningful and spiritual experience. People report enjoying the opportunity and flexibility to view or listen to the sermon while walking on the treadmill or commuting to work later in the week.

As described in Kay's book, *Being the Church in the Post-Pandemic World,* many churches pivoted to online worship for the first time at the beginning of the pandemic. The motivation to do so was primarily to serve the needs and desires of the already-gathered congregation. Because of that narrowed focus of the already-gathered rather than the broader focus of both the already-gathered and the yet-to-be-gathered community, hospitality and connection were either not a priority or were missing completely from the experience.

In addition, most churches again were too narrowly focused, thinking only of offering an online worship service. Many churches failed to think more broadly about the opportunities of offering online ministry—the full expression of a faith community in the digital world. The fuller expression could provide opportunities for discipleship, generosity, service, prayer, inviting others, etc.

In past eras, almost all faith formation occurred on Sunday mornings for all ages in the traditional Sunday school format. This has grown less and less common. Not only has the name and format changed, but so has the day. Now faith formation occurs in small groups in a variety of places and at all times of the day on different days of the week. It is no longer Sunday-centric in most churches.

Consider how Jesus spent his time. He didn't spend all his time at church or temple on Sundays. While he did spend some of his time at the temple, Jesus spent most of his time meeting with people every day out in the community and in their homes. He hung out where people were doing life.

While worship is typically about a one-hour experience on Sunday, this leaves 167 additional hours a week when the bulk of life happens. Jesus understood this and knew that to genuinely get to know people, He would need to share life experiences with them beyond the one-hour experience on Sunday. And Jesus wasn't totally sold on sabbath as demonstrated when He didn't even uphold the strict letter of the law when it came to the sabbath. Jesus was even accused of breaking the sabbath by pulling off the heads of grain to munch on them with his disciples and heal a man with a crippled hand (Matthew 12:1-14).

Hospitality Beyond Sunday

We often think of church hospitality as being welcoming and accommodating to people on Sunday mornings before, during, and after a worship service. While these elements are important for a meaningful worship experience, we usually leave the hospitality at the worship table and often forget to implement this same hospitality in our everyday interactions with people.

What would our communities look like if we were as welcoming and accommodating to people outside the Sunday worship experience? Think of your Sunday worship community like a table. There are certain expectations at that table. You say hello, greet, offer coffee, a pastry, show them to their seats, etc. But there are other tables within our communities: in our homes, places of business, where we shop, where we eat, etc. What if those tables where we are already gathering outside of Sunday mornings looked just as welcoming as our tables do for a worship experience on Sunday?

The Cost of Sunday-Centric

As leaders of the church, it is our responsibility to be good stewards of the tithes and offerings gifted to the church. We are to leverage those offerings in a way that provides the most missional outcome. In other words, church leaders are accountable to Jesus for assuring that the gifts given to the church are helping new people become acquainted with Jesus and helping existing disciples mature in becoming, knowing, and living more like Jesus.

How is your church evaluating its effectiveness in the purpose for which Jesus created the church as reflected below in Matthew 28:18-20 (also known as the Great Commission)? How well does your church do in aligning its resources for this purpose?

> *Jesus, undeterred, went right ahead and gave his charge: "God authorized and commanded me to commission you: Go out and train everyone you meet, far and near, in this way of life, marking them by baptism in the threefold name: Father, Son, and Holy Spirit. Then instruct them in the practice of all I have commanded you. I'll be with you as you do this, day after day after day, right up to the end of the age."*
>
> **Matthew 18-20 (MSG)**

Consider the full scope of your church's resources. Although not an exhaustive list, the following provides a good start in considering the full scope of the church's resources:

- Facility
- Grounds, parking lots
- Cost of utilities
- Cost of facility and grounds maintenance and upkeep
- Capital improvements to faculty and grounds

- Pastor(s)

- Staff

- Musicians & Vocalists

- Pastor(s) and staff benefits, including housing, pensions, benefits, and employer taxes

- Ministry Team Leaders

- Ministry Team Members

- Budget

- Endowment(s) and Benevolence(s)

- Congregation's time

- Congregation's energy

- Calendar of the church

- Equipment, furnishings, fixtures, and instruments

Once church leaders have a full grasp and inventory of the inclusive extent of your church's resources it has been blessed to receive, it is now time to complete some deep analysis. Challenge your leaders to process the following questions:

1. How many new people came to know Jesus last year through your church? What was the total budget of the church last year? Divide the budget by the number of new people. How much does it cost to introduce each new person to Jesus in the life of your church? Run this same formula for the past five to ten years. What is the trend you notice?

2. Evaluate how much of the budget is currently slated specifically to reach new people. If our mission is to reach new people, does the budget reflect this missional focus? Why or why not?

3. Next, consider how many resources are concentrated on the Sunday morning experience. How much of the pastor's time is spent focused on Sunday worship? Staff? What are those costs related to the overall staffing budget? How much time, energy, and focus do ministry team leaders and members use for the Sunday morning experience compared to other ministries?

4. How much of the equipment, fixtures, and instrument costs are geared for all—or mostly all—the Sunday morning experience?

5. Add up the total cost of dollars, time, energy, focus, and people invested in the Sunday morning experience (average of one to three hours). Compare this cost to how effective this investment is in introducing new people to Christ. How effective do you believe this investment is? How do you believe Jesus would rate it?

Relationally-Centric

*Imagine using stories to decenter Sunday as the focal point
of the church's ministry and instead put the emphasis on
how we are joining in God's work in the world.*

Jon Ritner[10]

To move away from being Sunday-centric means
we will need to move to more relationally-centric.
Instead of a specific time and day for calling the entire
congregation together, church ministry will focus on
relationships with one another, gathering/calling smaller
groups (communities) together routinely and the larger
congregation perhaps on a monthly basis.

In essence, a group commits to "do life together."
"Doing life together" will look different for each group,
but essentially, they will choose how to mature in
their spiritual walk together. The group will support,
encourage, and hold one another accountable for ongoing
faith formation. They will likely meet every week. During
those weekly times together, they might engage in one or
more of the following:

- Pray with one another

- Engage in accountability conversations (i.e., Where
  have you been able to follow Jesus this week, when
  has it been difficult to follow Jesus, and how will you
  get back on track?)

---

[10] Jon Ritner, *Positively Irritating: Embracing a Post-Christian World to Form a More Faithful & Innovative Church,* 100 Movements Publishing, 2020.

- Study the Bible together

- Share a meal (communion)

- Serve together

- Worship together (including singing)

Sunday Worship Service-Centric

Nevertheless, we turn to Scripture to find there is the Word of God and to remember.

We read Scripture in Christian community, not in the university, however helpful the scholarly tools and research may be.

In Christian community the practice of reading Scripture engages the church in discernment (instead of passive congregation).

Together we plot the story of Scripture. Together we talk and argue about how to interpret and shape our lives – and our common life – in remembrance. In that dialogue people must listen to

Scripture and to each other, muting neither Scripture nor each other.[11]

Allen D. Verhey

Some churches are moving away from weekly worship services. Instead they are practicing more of the "scattered" rather than the "gathered" model of church life. This is a more contemporary or postmodern approach

---

[11] Allen D. Verhey, *Remembering Jesus: Christian Community, Scripture, and the Moral Life*, Wm. B Eerdmans Publishing Co., 2005.

to spirituality where smaller groups of people would be in Christian community together. They would gather corporately less often or perhaps not at all. This approach moves the church away from being Sunday worship-centric to more spiritual community (small group) centric.

I (Michael) often ask people what "church" is to them. The most common answer I receive is that church is worship—usually a Sunday morning worship service. When I ask what "worship" is, I often get responses like, "It's praying, music, and preaching."

So, we now ask you the same question. What is worship? Worship services often involve people at altars. An altar is symbolic of a table. We meet God at an altar...a table...God's table. We see this for the first time in the Bible in Genesis 8:20 (NIV) after the flood waters recede: "Then Noah built an altar to the Lord and, taking some of all the clean animals and clean birds, he sacrificed burnt offerings on it." This is the first recorded "worship service" in the Bible. There is no music or praying or preaching. It is simply Noah, an altar, some dead birds, and the presence of God. This act is done in gratitude to God and involves sacrifice.

We see hundreds of these altars built throughout the Bible. This is how worship originates. No building, not on Sunday, no pastor, and no passing of an offering plate.

The theme of an ever-present altar without a building, pastor, passing of an offering plate or the requirement of a Sunday schedule continues until the time of Moses and the exodus of the Hebrew people out of Egypt. After the exodus from Egypt, Moses received instruction from God in what we call the Ten Commandments. These were holy and sacred. Then God instructs the people to build the Ark to house them in, a table, lamp stands, and several other things. God also instructed them to build a tent (a very large tent) to house all these items. In essence, the first church was built. This is where God was thought to reside, and it was mobile. Wherever the Israelites went, the tent, table, and Ark went with them. God was always with the people—in a tent. If you wanted to encounter God, you would go to the tent.

Once the people settled in Jerusalem, they built a temple for these sacred items. Now there was a permanent structure where God "resided." This temple not only housed the sacred artifacts but it was also the place one came to encounter God. This practice became routine in the Bible's Old Testament.

The first temple was destroyed, and another one was built. The second temple is the one we read about in Jesus's ministry where he goes and observes the widow giving her offering, and it is also where he flips over the money changers' tables because they are taking advantage of people.

Worship is meant to be about sacrifice and thankfulness, but people started to forget why they were worshiping (Isaiah 1:11-14). I (Michael) believe this is in our nature. When we do something as part of a routine, we often lose our understanding or memory of why we are doing it. Perhaps we act out of a sense of pattern, practice, or obligation rather than engage in this ritual for a deeper purpose or meaning. We sacrifice, pray, and worship so God can guide us to people who need our time, energy, and love.

Encounters with God (worship) originated as sacrifices at altars. These encounters moved into a tent, then a temple, and eventually, Jesus teaches us that God can be encountered anywhere. God is in all of us. We see this after Jesus' resurrection when He was with the disciples as they hid in a locked room. Jesus told them that He would be with them always and that He would leave them with a comforter. He then breathed on them. This breath is representative of the Holy Spirit. God is in our breath—in everything. God can be encountered at our dining room table, a conference table at work, a bar table in a local establishment—literally anywhere.

Story

When my wife, Stacy, and I (Michael) were on our second church plant in Blue Springs, Missouri, we often scheduled "happy hours" at local restaurants and pubs. This accomplished two things: it built relationships with local business owners and their employees, and it allowed us to have "spiritual" and "faith" conversations with people outside the "normal" Sunday morning experience.

I remember one of these experiences that happened

in 2019. We were at a local restaurant with a few friends who had invited their friends to share a drink and a few appetizers with us. We started with the usual pleasantries of who you are and what you do. I am always hesitant to share that I am a pastor, but it most always eventually comes out. Per the usual response, the new friends immediately apologized for cursing and pushed their drink away. I respond with, "I'm not that kind of pastor."

We moved through the evening, and twenty minutes later, my daughter sent me a picture of herself all dressed up for a school dance. As a proud papa, I showed it to everyone at the table. As I did this, one of our new friends looked at me and yelled straight into my face, "That is not okay!" I was completely taken off guard. What is not okay? My daughter? Was there something protruding out of her head that I missed? I quickly looked at the photo; thankfully, I hadn't missed anything. She yells again, "That is not okay!" I responded, "What is not okay"? She points out that my daughter's dress is inappropriate for a pastor's kids—or any kid—to wear in public.

In this moment, something begins to well up inside of me. Some of you may have experienced this feeling. You may call it the unleashing of papa bear. Her dress was fine. She looked beautiful. How dare you judge my daughter. The next few moments were what I call "God" moments. I was about to set this woman straight when my wonderful wife stopped me and saved my reputation as a pastor. She looked at the woman and said, "Tell me more about why you feel this is inappropriate." I literally turned around and made new friends at a different table.

An hour later, my wife and this woman were the only two left, and they were talking about deep, spiritual topics. The woman had grown up being told that God only loved her if she wore certain clothes or acted a certain way. By the end of the night, we had a two-hour church service...in a bar...on a Tuesday night. My experience is that more "church" happens during the week in our average, mundane life experiences than it does on Sunday mornings.

Evaluation

How Sunday-centric is your church? Consider the topics below and rate your church on how Sunday-centric each topic/area is on a scale of zero (not at all Sunday-centric) to ten (completely Sunday-centric).

Worship

0   1   2   3   4   5   6   7   8   9   10

Discipleship

0   1   2   3   4   5   6   7   8   9   10

Hospitality

0   1   2   3   4   5   6   7   8   9   10

Service

0   1   2   3   4   5   6   7   8   9   10

Building New Relationships

0   1   2   3   4   5   6   7   8   9   10

Percentage of Staffing Time Used

0   1   2   3   4   5   6   7   8   9   10

Percentage of Staffing Dollars Investment

0   1   2   3   4   5   6   7   8   9   10

Usage of Servant Hours

0   1   2   3   4   5   6   7   8   9   10

Overall Percentage of the Budget

0   1   2   3   4   5   6   7   8   9   10

Usage of the Building

0   1   2   3   4   5   6   7   8   9   10

Percentage of Building Dollars Investment

0   1   2   3   4   5   6   7   8   9   10

Overall Sunday-Centric

0   1   2   3   4   5   6   7   8   9   10

Questions

1. What new information did you discover in this chapter? How is it resonating with your idea of "church"?

2. What ideas are you struggling with most from the shift away from a Sunday-centric church? What is the underlying fear behind this struggle?

3. How would the life of your church be different if people in their twenties and thirties were involved? How different would the church need to look for this to become a reality?

4. What will your prayers be tonight as you process this chapter?

5. As a church leader, how will you bravely and courageously lead your church to reach new people in your context?

CHAPTER TWO
Moving Away from Building-Centric

*As you sent me into the world, so I have
sent them into the world.*

John 17:18 (CEB)

The worship model set by Jesus was nothing like worship in the modern church. Jesus did not expect people to come to him on a particular day at the temple. Instead, Jesus went to the people. Consider where Jesus spent his time and did most of his ministry. Again, it was not hanging out at the temple.

Jesus ate meals with many people in their homes (Luke 10:38-42, John 12:2, Mark 2:15). He hung out with people where they were doing life, going about their common daily tasks, like collecting water. Jesus attended festivities and special occasions such as weddings (John 2:1-12). He met the Samaritan woman at the well (John 4:7-42) and met the tax collector Zacchaeus while traveling through Jericho and then ate dinner in his home (Luke 19:1-10). He met the disabled man at the pools in Bethzatha (John 5:1-15). He met the hemorrhaging woman near Gerasenes

(Mark 5: 24-34). Jesus even called his disciples in their workplaces, like the fishermen (Matthew 4:18-22) and Matthew, the tax collector (Matthew 9:9). Jesus entered their hearts through their sacred spaces, times, and events.

Wesley and Paul Take to the Streets

The founder of Methodism, John Wesley, started his preaching in "open-air" in 1739 after being refused access to the pulpit at Epworth by George Whitfield. Wesley realized that preaching in the open air greatly benefited him and, ultimately, the Methodist movement. Being outside meant that there were no limits on building size or seating. He could literally go to any public place and start preaching. It was not uncommon for Wesley to gather three thousand or more people at a time. Not once did he assign a particular place and time for people to gather to hear him preach. He preached in public gathering places, and as people happened to be in the area and heard him, they leaned into his message because he grabbed their attention.

The Apostle Paul also did much of his ministry outside the church. He made three missionary journeys (some would report four missionary journeys) through Antioch, Cyprus, Lystra, Syria, Cilicia, Derbe, Galatia, Phrygia, Philippi, Thessalonica, Berea, Athens, Corinth, Ephesus, Jerusalem, Rome, Macedonia, Achaia, Greece, Troas, Assos, Mitylene, Chios, and Miletus as documented in the Book of Acts. Paul's travels and ministries are documented in the thirteen books of the Bible he authored in the New Testament.

Third places are the most significant places for Christian mission to occur because in a third place people are more relaxed, less guarded, more open to meaningful conversation and interaction.

Michael Frost
Exiles: Living Missionally in a Post-Christian Culture

Paul also spent time in people's homes and businesses. When Paul went to Corinth, he discovered Aquila, a Jew born in Pontus, and his wife, Priscilla. They had just arrived from Italy, part of the general expulsion of Jews from Rome ordered by Claudius. Paul moved in with them, and they worked together at their common trade of tent-making. But every Sabbath, he was at the meeting place, trying his best to convince both Jews and Greeks about Jesus (Acts 18:1-3). During this passage, Paul was preaching and simultaneously demonstrating how to share faith in the marketplace. He was doing life alongside people where they spent the majority of their time—in their place of business.

Not Theological or Historical

Where does this building-centric approach to American church come from? We have already explored that Jesus's approach to ministry was certainly not building-centric, nor was the Apostle Paul's or John Wesley's. So how have we arrived at such a place where we are so building-centric and even building-dependent for ministry to occur?

Back in the early times of the American colonies, there was one community building. This one community building, often referred to as the "meetinghouse," is where all community business took place and also where worship was conducted. It was a shared space for any gatherings of the community. In the 17th and early 18th centuries, separating the secular and spiritual was unheard of as they saw these two aspects intertwined into everyday life. Because of this understanding, the common meetinghouse approach to serve all community gatherings worked well for everyone for decades.

It was only when some thought that a few of the secular meetings were getting out of hand that the church decided the secular meetings needed to move elsewhere. The church reasoned it needed to have its own "sacred" space separate from secular space, and so the secular gatherings were kicked out of the meetinghouses. The utilitarian buildings then began to morph into more of the churches built in the 19th and 20th centuries. A domed ceiling was originally added for better sound, but it later became a symbol of heaven. A steeple was added, and later a cross was affixed to the steeple. The meetinghouse door was relocated to the end, and the pulpit was moved to the opposite end facing the rising sun.

Now go back and reread the previous paragraph. The church kicked the community out of the building. No longer were neighbors allowed to gather where they had gathered for decades. The church set itself apart and forfeited its immersion in the culture. Once enmeshed with the heartbeat of the community, the church chose to detach itself. What a church wouldn't do to be amid such activity today.

While the church often blames the government for the "separation of church and state," the church kicked the citizens out of the community's gathering place. It was as if, at that very moment, we were already messaging to the community that only perfect people can enter here. No behavior that isn't Godly can take place in this space. We can't disagree, and we can't be loud or have spirited conversations. Maybe this is when the church should have been challenged to be a hospital for sinners, not a museum for saints.

Historian Kevin Sweeney notes,[12] "As the sanctity of exclusively religious space grew, (the church) grew more marginal in the shared public life of communities where commerce, politics, and other cultural activities increased in importance."

Even John Wesley warned those gathered at the 1784 Christmas Conference about spending too much on church buildings:

Let all our chapels be built plain and decent;
but not more expensively than is absolutely avoidable:
Otherwise the Necessity of raising Money
Will make Rich Men necessary to us.

---

[12] Kevin Sweeney, *Meetinghouses,Townhouses, and Churches: Changing Perceptions of Sacred and Secular Space in Southern New England,* 1993.

But if so, we must be dependent upon them,
yea, and governed by them.
And then farewell to the Methodist-Discipline,
if not Doctrine, too.[13]

By 1824, the statement had been revised, and the words "and with free seats" was placed right after "plain and decent." This phrase was added because other denominations had adopted a pew rental system to pay for church buildings, making social hierarchy a reality and creating a church with clear economic status requirements. While some Methodists wanted to keep up with the Presbyterian and Congregational churches in their communities, this addition was meant to keep the Methodist churches from falling into the same trap.

Unfortunately, Wesley's statement and values regarding buildings from 1784 slowly eroded over time. This turn is greatly contributed to Bishop Matthew Simpson, who was elected to the episcopacy in 1852. Simpson often gloated about the growing number of "better class" church buildings and even more about the rising values of the buildings. He "never expressed concern that a church was too expensive, elaborately adorned, or large." Instead, he referenced them as "handsome and commodious churches" that fell well

---

[13] Kevin M. Watson, *Embodying Methodist Theology: Diverging Conceptions of Holy Living in American Methodist Theology; Prepublication copy of a chapter from Old or New School Methodism? The Fragmentation of a Theological Tradition,* (Oxford University Press, forthcoming) https://https://oimts.files.wordpress.com/2018/11/2018-05-watson.pdf.

outside Wesley's description of church buildings.

Benjamin Titus ("B.T.") Roberts was highly critical of Bishop Simpson and his value on church buildings and the Methodist Episcopal Church's (MEC) increasing awareness of its own prosperity and influence. Roberts felt Methodism was drifting away from Wesley's convictions on how best to "raise a holy people." B.T. wrote about "Old and New School Methodism." This provides a description of the fault lines of the old and new Methodist ways:

> *Differing thus in their view of religion,*
> *the Old and New School Methodists necessarily*
> *differ in their measures for its promotion.*
> *The latter build stock churches, and furnish them*
> *with pews to accommodate a select congregation;*
> *with organs, melodeons, violins, and*
> *professional singers, to execute difficult pieces*
> *of music for a fashionable audience.*
> *The former favor free churches, congregational*
> *singing, and spirituality, spread of the gospel upon the*
> *agency of the Holy Ghost, and the purity of the Church.*
> *The New School Methodists appear to depend*
> *upon the patronage of the worldly,*
> *the favor of the proud, aspiring;*
> *and the various artifices of worldly policy.*[14]

B.T. Roberts described the tensions between the new and old Methodism "beneath the spectacular prospering of the MEC with regard to people, building, and general

---

[14] Benjamin Titus Roberts letter to Bishop Thomas Morris, Nov. 15, 1856.

upward mobility." Roberts was eventually expelled from the MEC and formed the Free Methodist Church of North America denomination in 1860. He went on to found a publication, *The Earnest Christian,* and Chili Seminary (now named Roberts Wesleyan College) in New York.[15] The Free Methodist Church is known for its help with the Underground Railroad.

Perhaps Roberts was one of the first to see the writing on the proverbial walls of how the focus on buildings—let alone the insider focus on people—would eventually lead to the demise of many churches. Maybe Roberts was one of the first "APEs" (see a full explanation on this subject in Chapter 3) to leave the "building" and the institution of the day.

People Over Property

Bishop Kenneth H. Carter, Jr. and Reverend Audrey Warren offer wise insights in their book, *Fresh Expressions of People Over Property.* Their insights include:

- By and large, most churches spend more on their buildings than they do on people (p.12).

- The sacred symbol is only as strong as the authenticity of the people bearing the symbol (p. 23).

- Places are sacred because they are made so by human beings (p. 26).

---

15   https://en.wikipedia.org/wiki/B._T._Roberts.

- In John 2:19-22, Jesus said, "Destroy the temple and in three days I'll raise it up." Jesus was referencing destroying a temple (building) but raising up His body (p. 29).

- A healthy view of church property embraces the idea that sacred space is useful yet also transcended by the collective body of Christ when fulfilling God's mission in a local community (p. 29).

- For the existing church building to maintain its space, it must blend holy time and human time (p. 32).

- A place is holy because people share a community purpose for living life as disciples. As stewards of holy space, we are accountable for whether the space transforms the people inside of it and beyond the four walls (p. 34).

- What is healthy for our community and our neighbors is healthy for our church (p. 60).

These authors not only offer wise words about navigating the difficult topic and task of church property, but they also tackle some tough, complicated, and complex projects. I (Kay) have had the privilege of journeying with Pastor Audrey through part of her project at First United Methodist Church of Miami. She, along with other strong congregational laity leaders, navigated selling their property to a commercial developer, moving to a temporary location while a 49-story building is built with

639 units named "Society." The church will own 25,000 square feet in the building on four multi-story floors, including a three-story sanctuary overlooking Biscayne Boulevard and the Atlantic Ocean.

First UMC of Miami leveraged its downtown property and placed itself right in the middle of a community. The space was designed with the people who will be living in the building in mind. A free-trade coffee bar is open to the public on the first floor where relationships can be built with people in the building and others in the neighborhood. There is a flexible space that can be used for social gatherings, basketball, a climbing wall, volleyball, small banquets, and more. Staffing is also structured to connect with those in the building as well as the congregation.

This brave and courageous decision has positioned the church for a solid financial future and allowed it to experiment with innovative ministries. First UMC of Miami already has a strong ministry for the under-housed called "The Breakfast Club." In addition, they have expanded to offer a community theater. Many more ministries are planned and will be implemented over the next few years. All of this is possible because these leaders placed people over property.

Everting Discipleship-Making

The future requires us to replace our industrial disciple making approach with one that equips individuals to make disciples outside of our factory's four walls. For that, we must restructure our disciple making pathway by actually reversing its flow.

Jon Ritner
Positively Irritating: Embracing a Post-Christian World to Form a More Faithful & Innovative Church

Most churches conduct their disciple-making activities inside their buildings. For instance, worship is held in the building. Sunday School is taught in the building. The quilting group gets together at the church. The administrative council meets in the church's boardroom. Ministry teams/committees convene at the church. The potluck dinner is held in the fellowship hall. Even donated items for community mission projects are collected at the church facility before being delivered to a service agency in the community.

Church members often struggle with leaving the church facility and grounds to build relationships with the neighbors. The inherent desire and expectation are that the neighbors should come to the church (the building) instead of the church (the people) going into the community. Even though the age of Christendom (a time when the majority of the population was made up of Christians) ended in the mid-1960s, many churches, even sixty years later, still conduct themselves as though we still live in this type of culture. They have yet to realize that Christians are now the minority population. Until this realization is faced, the church will continue to struggle to make the required shifts to meet the culture and the people who reside amongst it, let alone have the opportunity to share their faith.

Taking the Church Online

According to a recent Barna study, "Six Questions About the Future of the Hybrid Church Experience," only 41 percent of Gen Z say that, when COVID is over, they want to return to primarily in-person worship, and only 42 percent of Millennials say they prefer primarily in-person worship. This means, of course, that the majority do not prefer in-person worship.

When considering taking the church online, we must think beyond the Sunday morning experience. In other words, we have to think beyond simply placing a recording of the worship service in the sanctuary online to be viewed later in the week. Instead, to truly take church online, we must consider an online ministry approach rather than only online worship. What would the full expression of online ministry look like in your context? A full expression would need to include worship, hospitality, connection, discipleship for all ages, service, prayer, generosity, and leadership.

People's interest in engaging in online ministry is not going away. Online ministry was not a stopgap only for the pandemic. It is a vital ministry method for the present-day church and the church of the future. For churches doing online ministry well, it is increasingly becoming a vital method of reaching people who would otherwise likely be unreachable. According to Lifeway Research, 53 percent of people attending church watched more online services in 2020 than in 2019. Barna reported that 53 percent of practicing Christians streamed their churches online. Another interesting statistic, according to Vimeo Livestream, is that 33 percent of parishioners discovered their church online. Forty-five percent of Americans watched an online service in 2021. Of those who watched, 15 percent were not people who normally attended church.[16]

How much is your church investing in your online ministry? How much is your church investing in your onsite ministry? What percentages of the budget and asset usage does this represent of both? How missionally effective is each?

What if we deployed the church to invite its neighbors to its virtual ministry table?

In 2020, for the first time, more Americans listened to podcasts weekly (24%) than physically attended church services weekly (23%).[17]

The pandemic opened a whole new world to people and demonstrated there are options. Now people like and

---

[16] https://webtribunal.net/blog/online-church-statistics/#gref.

[17] https://comparecamp.com/church-attendance-statistics/.

expect options and flexibility. I (Kay) recently conducted an out-of-state workshop. Churches were asked to attend in small groups with their pastor. There were about sixty-five people sitting in the room with me, and more than a hundred people connected virtually in nineteen different locations. Some small groups gathered in their church remotely. Some small group members connected from their individual homes but were placed in their own group's virtual breakout room for small group discussion during breakout sessions. Other small groups had some in the room and some connecting from their homes. While it made the coordination on the technology side a bit more complex, people appreciated the option to connect in a way that worked best for them.

Reaching Generation Z

According to Dillon Smith, a staffer at Carey Nieuwhof Communications, these are seven habits of Gen Z that the church might be ignoring and therefore likely causing issues in connecting with this young generation:[18]

1. Gen Z watches whatever they want when they want. The options are too great to waste time viewing or doing things they don't want to view or do.

2. Before a person of Gen Z will trust you, they need to get to know you. It is important to offer more personal content to build up trust.

---

[18] https://careynieuwhof.com/7-habits-of-generation-z-that-your-church-might-be-ignoring/.

3. Considered the "me-centered" generation, in order to reach them, the church needs to let them know what's in it for them, what impact can be made, and how to join the movement.

4. Gen Z does/will not hang out on the same social media platforms as their parents. The church will likely need to invest in new platforms and invest in Gen Z staff or volunteers with decision-making power and authority in order to reach their own generation.

5. Diversity is not optional. This generation has grown up in diversity and expects it. The church needs to be at least as diverse as the school they attend(ed).

6. Mental health is a huge issue and isn't going away. The church needs to have a regular focus on mental health and wellness.

7. It is important to understand that when talking to non-Christian friends about church, most of the Gen Z population feel they need to first lead with an apology for the church (even though they had nothing to do with it) and convince others that not every Christian is judgmental or abusive before they can have a spiritual conversation with another person of their generation.

This is a sobering list, right? These Gen Zs are young people born between 1997 and 2012 and are often referred to as the "Digital-ites" or "Zoomers." They are known for constantly being connected and messaging on the Internet, social media, or mobile systems. While the generation ahead of them, the Millennials, makes up 25 percent of the total population, Gen Z is now the largest population at 27 percent.[19] Together, these two generations now comprise more than half the population and are the most missing demographic in the church. Considering that 59 percent of Millennials who were born with a religious affiliation tend to unplug from their church and 45 percent of Gen Z say they rarely or never attend church,[20] the church needs to make some radical adjustments to once again be compelling and relevant to these generations.

The Millennials and Gen Zs are not hanging out in church buildings and are not likely to be attracted to the ministries going on inside most churches today. The research reveals two important findings:

1. Millennials and Gen Zs are the most unchurched generations.
2. These two generations hang out on online platforms.

The problem is that most of our churches are struggling to gain ground—let alone be competent and compelling—when using technology and online platforms. Herein lies the great divide! (These findings do not even address the youngest generation, the Alpha Generation, born after 2010, who are even more digitally dependent.)

We need to actively create an authentic community

---

[19] https://www.insiderintelligence.com/insights/generation-z-facts/.

[20] https://comparecamp.com/church-attendance-statistics/.

where these generations can find a sense of belonging and purpose and where they can have a meaningful impact on the world and make a difference.

Story

In the late spring/early summer of 2020, as the world was shutting down from the COVID-19 pandemic, a need arose in our community to help get food to children in need. Children who were food-insecure normally received their lunch at school, so after schools shut down that spring—and then into the summer—the meals continued to be made available at the schools. The problem was that the meals were only accessible to those who had transportation to and from the school to pick them up, and many of the food-insecure families did not have access to transportation during the day to get those meals.

Someone at our church who worked for the school district came to us and asked if we could help distribute those meals to the food-insecure neighborhoods. So, we teamed up with the school district and helped provide food, packed it, and then distributed the meals. From this initiative, the Blue Springs summer lunch program was born.

One of these neighborhoods incorporates a group of hotels on the north side of town where a large homeless population resides. These people are food-, money-, and general-resource insecure. We not only serve meals in the summer, but we also have "block parties" in the fall where we make burgers and hot dogs and drink hot chocolate.

We also bring boxes of socks, underwear, coats, and gloves to allow people to "shop" for their needs.

One time another pastor was there and approached me (Michael) with a small book. It was one of the gospels— Matthew, I think. He asked me what I was doing, and I said, "We are eating and shopping with our friends today." He told me he was handing out the gospel, to which I replied, "So are we."

This gospel was "handed out" or "spread" not in a church but at a hotel—in a parking lot. How much spreading of the gospel do we actually do inside our church buildings? Does your church have a food pantry? Great! What if you were to take that food to the people who needed it instead of expecting people to come to your food pantry? This is how the expansion of the gospel (the Good News) works. You take it to the people. You deliver it where the people are already doing life: in their places of work, neighborhoods, restaurants, parks...the list goes on and on.

Evaluation

How building-centric is your church? Consider the topics below and rate your church on how building-centric each topic/area is on a scale of zero (not at all building-centric) to ten (completely building-centric). What percentage of the activities within each area are conducted inside your building versus outside (or online) your building? For example, if you only offer worship in the sanctuary of your church building, you would score ten.

Worship

0   1   2   3   4   5   6   7   8   9   10

Discipleship

0   1   2   3   4   5   6   7   8   9   10

Hospitality

0   1   2   3   4   5   6   7   8   9   10

Service

0   1   2   3   4   5   6   7   8   9   10

Building New Relationships

0   1   2   3   4   5   6   7   8   9   10

Staffing Time

0   1   2   3   4   5   6   7   8   9   10

Staffing Dollars

0   1   2   3   4   5   6   7   8   9   10

Usage of Servant Hours

0   1   2   3   4   5   6   7   8   9   10

Overall % of the Budget

0   1   2   3   4   5   6   7   8   9   10

Evangelism

0   1   2   3   4   5   6   7   8   9   10

Fellowship

0   1   2   3   4   5   6   7   8   9   10

Overall Building-Centric

0   1   2   3   4   5   6   7   8   9   10

Questions

1. How do you spread the gospel in your building? Is it working/effective?

2. How do you spread the gospel outside your building? Is it working/effective?

3. How do you, or how can you, spread the gospel at your place of work? Is it working/effective?

4. How do you, or how can you, spread the gospel in your neighborhood? Is it working/effective?

5. What are the mundane tasks of your weekly life? How can you incorporate the spreading of the gospel through those tasks?

CHAPTER THREE
Moving Away from Pastor-Centric

So I give you a new command:
Love each other deeply and fully.
Remember the ways that I have loved you,
and demonstrate your love for
others in those same ways.

John 13:34 (VOICE)

I believe a hierarchical form of church leadership is
oppressive to the rest of the church body. It is, in essence, a
form of "Spiritual Munchausen by Proxy" - a medical term
for a condition in which a parent becomes so enmeshed
in the care of a sick child that, even as the child's health
begins to improve, the parent deliberately keeps the child
ill. The parent's sense of value and identity is so closely
tied to his or her role as the caregiver that he or she "needs
to be needed" by the child in order to have purpose in life.

John Ritner.[21]

The Methodist movement was founded as a laity
movement with initial explosive and expansive growth.

---

[21] Jon Ritner, *Positively Irritating: Embracing a Post-Christian World to Form a More Faithful & Innovative Church,* 100 Movements Publishing, 2020.

Unfortunately, as the requirements for education and the professionalization of clergy expanded, the equipping, empowering, and mobilizing of laity greatly decreased and has ultimately diminished the church's impact on the community and the Kingdom.

Wesley is famous for this quote:

> *Give me one hundred preachers who fear nothing but sin, and desire nothing but God, and I care not a straw whether they be clergy or laymen [women], such alone will shake the gates of hell and set up the kingdom of heaven upon the earth.*

According to Roger Finke and Rodney Stark, sociologists and educators, "The dramatic metric rise of the Methodists was short-lived. It is instructive to note that the Methodists began to slump precisely when their amateur clergy were replaced by professionals who claimed episcopal authority over their congregations."

Wesley was a fan and promoter of laity, as shared in his sermon entitled, "A Caution against Bigotry," in which he highlighted the importance and support of the lay preacher's ministry:

> *Beware how you attempt to hinder him (her/the layperson), either by your authority, or arguments, or persuasions. Do not in anywise strive to prevent his (her) using all the power which God has given him (her). If you have authority with him (her), do not use that authority to stop the work of God.*

Creating Unintentional Limitations

Men and women are not ordained
to this ministerial priesthood
in order to take priesthood
away from the people
but in order to nourish and
sustain the priesthood of the people.

Lesslie Newbigin

Clergy-centric churches limit ministry potential when they become dependent on one person. When every detail of every ministry must flow through one person, we become constrained in our ministry capacity. Thus, the rate a ministry can run efficiently declines.

Organizations tend to be operated from the top down. Many secular organizational charts look like a pyramid instead of a bar graph, and churches are very similar. Often the pastor(s) in a clergy-centric church creates a bottleneck in the organization because the organization is limited to the abilities and capacities of the pastor(s) or leadership team(s).

John Ritner shares:

New expressions of church require that pastoral leaders identify and renounce elements of the existing culture that foster dependence on professionals, and instead encourage a culture of permission granting, power sharing, and dream awakening. We continually remind our staff that our role is not to do the ministry of the church, but to equip others to engage in God's mission in the ways he is leading them.[22]

---

[22] ibid.

Not only does the church need to move away from being pastor-centric, but it also needs to move away from being staff-centric. Too often, church leaders want a ministry area to grow, so they hire someone to "do" the ministry for them. This is not the intended purpose of staff nor is this a healthy practice. When staff does the ministry for the disciples, the growth and maturity of disciples are stunted, and they become dependent and privileged instead of developing a servant's heart, attitude, and maturity. Otherwise, the dependence cycle is perpetuated. Bishop Kennon L. Callahan declares, "The age of the professional pastor is over, and the age of missional pastor has begun."[23]

> *I have a lot more to say about this, but it is hard to get it across to you since you've picked up this bad habit of not listening. By this time you ought to be teachers yourselves, yet here I find you need someone to sit down with you and go over the basics on God again, starting from square one—baby's milk, when you should have been on solid food long ago! Milk is for beginners, inexperienced in God's ways; solid food is for the mature, who have some practice in telling right from wrong.*
>
> *Instead of doing the work of the church they developed and deployed people to do the work themselves.*

Hebrews 5:11-14, MSG

Whether it is the pastor, staff, or ministry team leaders, the focus and primary task is to identify, recruit, equip, and deploy disciples into ministry. Each one of

---

[23] Kennon L. Callahan, *Effective Church Leadership: Building on the Twelve Keys,* Harper and Row, 1990.

these leaders needs to have a layperson with them each time they engage in ministry so they can utilize the experience as an opportunity to equip, nurture, and encourage a disciple in ministry. This also eliminates the expectation that the pastor or staff member will always be the one out front. The pastor and staff become the model/equipper in the areas of congregational care, stewardship/fundraising, and building new relationships in the community. For most churches, this will require a dramatic shift in culture. Without this shift, the cycle will not be broken, and a new movement of deployed disciples will not take hold.

This dramatic shift everts the current church model. What if the church staff focused on training people to deploy to their own tables? Imagine the possibilities and how many new people could be reached if this became a reality for the majority of churches.

The moment you hand power over to other people, you get an explosion of curiosity, innovation, and effort.

Joshua Cooper Ramo
The Age of the Unthinkable

The Ultimate Equipper

Jesus was the ultimate equipper. In fact, He was a brilliant team equipper. Jesus tells the disciples that they will do even greater things than he did:

Believe me: I am in my Father and my Father is in me. If
you can't believe that, believe what you see—these works.
The person who trusts me will not only do what I'm doing
but even greater things, because I, on my way to the Father,
am giving you the same work to do that I've been doing.

John 14:11-12 (MSG)

Jesus did most of his teaching like he did his ministry. He did not gather his disciples into a classroom or temple and teach them theory. No! Jesus' disciples walked and traveled with him as he went about his ministry. They observed, and he would explain what and why he said or did what he did. He encouraged them and asked them to help (i.e., the feeding of the five thousand in Matthew 14:18-21). Then he sent them out on their own (Luke 9:1-6). He was the perfect mentor and demonstrated a great process to follow:

- I do. You watch. We talk.
- I do. You help. We talk.
- You do. I help. We talk.
- You do. I watch. We talk.
- You do. I go and identify a new disciple to mentor.

Too often, we spend so much time and energy begging people to serve that we leave no time for equipping and mentoring. This leaves people feeling undervalued and ill-equipped for ministry. When the church is unwilling to spend time training or mentoring, we send the message that the ministry is not worthy of such investment. In essence, the church is messaging that the ministry is not of value.

Community Developer

In United Methodism, a pastor, in theory, is appointed to a community instead of a church. Yet, in practice, the average pastor spends the vast majority of her/his time inside the building with people from the congregation. It is difficult not to get sucked into the vortex of this model and the expectation that the pastor is appointed to "care for the flock." In fact, most of the education and training a pastor receives reinforces this practice and use of time. It is not uncommon for a pastor to be taught to spend fifteen to twenty hours a week preparing a sermon and coordinating the worship experience. By the time the pastor attends all the committee meetings required of them and visits all the shut-ins, there is no time left to spend in the community. Then we wonder why the church is not growing and why there is a gap in cultural relevance.

If the church becomes less Sunday-centric, building-centric, and pastor-centric, this will allow the pastor to take on a much different role—the role of an equipper as we have already noted. In addition to becoming an equipper of disciples, the pastor shifts from being a congregational caregiver to a community developer. As a community developer, the pastor can embrace the greater idea of being appointed to a community with presence, participation, and impact. The pastor becomes a bridge-builder between the church and the community. The pastor develops a better understanding of the needs, gaps, and opportunities within the community and how the church can better intersect. In addition, the pastor will have real-life stories of lives and circumstances in the unchurched community to weave into sermons, bringing relevance and understanding to the churched community. This authenticity is one piece that has been missing from most faith communities for several decades. When a pastor can adopt this mindset AND mentor others, too, the possibilities are endless.

What would our communities look like if EVERYONE at our faith community tables felt empowered to create their own community around their different tables within their spheres of influence?

It Takes Everyone, Every Disciple

*Is it not true that the One who climbed up
also climbed down, down to the valley of earth?
And the One who climbed down
is the One who climbed back up,
up to the highest heaven.
He handed out gifts above and below,
filled heaven with his gifts,
filled earth with his gifts.
He handed out gifts of apostle, prophet,
evangelist, and pastor-teacher to train
Christ's followers in skilled servant work,
working within Christ's body, the church,
until we're all moving rhythmically
and easily with each other,*

efficient and graceful in response to God's Son,
fully mature adults, fully developed within and without,
fully alive like Christ.
No prolonged infancies among us, please.
We'll not tolerate babes in the woods,
small children who are easy prey for predators.
God wants us to grow up,
to know the whole truth and tell it in love—
like Christ in everything.
We take our lead from Christ,
who is the source of everything we do.
He keeps us in step with each other.
His very breath and blood flow through us,
nourishing us so that we will grow up healthy in God,
robust in love.

Ephesians 4:11-16 (MSG)

It takes the whole congregation to do God's work, for there is much ministry to be done. As Ephesians reminds us, each individual contributes a unique giftedness. It's both this unique, rich blend and the full spectrum of gifts that can offer the most comprehensive ministry for the community. When parts and gifts are missing or not fully developed, we cannot reach our potential and offer the full spectrum of ministry and impact God intended not only for one another, but for the community.

When we do not disciple the congregants well and fully, we end up with immature disciples still looking to be fed instead of mature disciples willing to feed others. In many of our churches, we have educated our people, but we have not discipled them. Maybe they know the stories of the Bible, but they have not had a transformational experience in their maturation of discipleship that creates a desire to participate in disciple-making. This shows up most apparently when existing (sometimes long-tenured) congregants' preferences repeatedly and continuously take center stage over reaching new people. Other ways this lack of discipling shows up is when congregants have been taught that discipleship equals showing up on Sunday for worship, throwing a buck in the plate, attending the fellowship time in their Sunday school, and taking care of their building. They have indeed been faithful to these four expectations, but it has not resulted in mature disciple-making disciples.

> *In the biblical sense all Christians are priests and clergy, and this is a crucial starting point if we are to re-discover the true concept of ministry and leadership within the church.*
>
> **David Watson**

Even understanding that each person has particular spiritual gifts, the church still struggles with the responsibilities and authority of the "called" professionals versus the laity. Eugene Peterson offers these thoughtful insights:

> *Within the Christian community, few words are more disabling than "layperson" and "laity." The words convey the impression—an impression that quickly solidifies into a lie—that there is a two-level hierarchy among the men and women who follow Jesus. There are those who are trained, sometimes referred to as "the called," the professionals*

who are paid to preach, teach, and provide guidance in the Christian way, occupying the upper level. The lower level is made up of everyone else, those whom God assigned jobs as storekeepers, lawyers, journalists, parents, and computer programmers.[24]

> *In the New Testament*
> *there are functional distinctions*
> *between various kinds of ministries*
> *but no hierarchical division*
> *between clergy and laity.*

> **Howard Snyder**

All are called by God, not just a few or not some special ones called to serve higher purposes. We are all called. In 1 Corinthians we are reminded:

> *Now there are many kinds of grace gifts, but they are all from the same Spirit. There are many different ways to serve, but they're all directed by the same Lord. There are many amazing working gifts in the church, but it is the same God who energizes them all in all who have the gifts.*

> **1 Corinthians 12:4-6 (VOICE)**

Alan Hirsch introduced the APEST five-fold model in his book, *The Forgotten Ways,* in 2009. APEST points to the Ephesians 4 reference that God hands out the gifts of apostle, prophet, evangelist, shepherd, and teacher. (Some would argue that it should be a four-fold process where a shepherd and teacher are linked together instead of being gifted separately.) Regardless of whether you take the

---

[24] Eugene Peterson, *The Jesus Way: A Conversation on the Ways Jesus Is the Way.*

four-fold or five-fold view, we must admit that the APEs (apostles, prophets, and evangelists) have, by and large, left the institutional church mostly out of frustration and because they felt undervalued. The innovators, pioneers, and visionaries are no longer present. Instead, these people often enter the nonprofit world to live out their ministry outside the institutional confines. Because of the church's rigidity and lack of innovation, creativity, and vision, the APEs find it difficult to function within the institutional constraints, and the institutional leaders often find the APEs difficult to manage because they do not always "play by the rules."

Like anything else, each role has its unique set of strengths and challenges. Here is a brief definition of each:[25]

- The Apostle: "One who is sent and extends"
- The Prophet: "One who questions and reforms"
- The Evangelist: "One who recruits and gathers"
- The Shepherd: "One who protects and provides"
- The Teacher: "One who understands and explains"

Reflect on the characteristics of each of these important and distinct roles described above again. Each role and function is vital. While many leaders and congregants remain in the church who protect, provide, understand, and explain, the church is left without nearly

---

[25] https://www.missionalchurchnetwork.com/blog/the-importance-of-5-fold-apest.

enough of those who send, extend, question, reform, recruit, and gather. Shepherds and teachers pacify and do no harm. Apostles, prophets, and evangelists are the ones who challenge, innovate, and reach new people. Our institutional systems have evolved to the point of primarily attracting and retaining shepherds and teachers while running off APEs.

God created a full expression of giftedness through a variety of people because the church needs ALL these gifts. It is only when ALL the people representing ALL these God-given gifts are present that the church can then be its intended and fullest expression with all its capabilities. For us to return to this much-needed, complete reflection that God intended, we need to completely reimagine how we order the church, equip disciples, use resources (including people's time, energy, and passions), and deploy disciples for the purposes God intended.

Imagine a faith community where apostles, prophets, evangelists, shepherds, and teachers are collectively called to gather at the same table and then uniquely deployed to serve in their giftedness. What a movement and impact that would be indeed.

Story

I (Michael) identify as an Enneagram 3. This means that I feel valued and loved when "I" accomplish things. Many "successful" pastors are often really good at doing things. Really good "doers of things" can benefit an organization but only in the short term. In order to maintain long-term success, pastors like myself must figure out how to train and deploy the many servants around us.

This realization hit me in the first year of our second church plant. We acquired an existing church building the year before we launched. I spent an entire year renovating, planning big events, going door to door, and building relationships in the community, all while serving our sister church in the next town over. And by "serving," I mean being responsible for organizing six worship services every week while also preaching two of those services...EVERY WEEK. My "Enneagram 3" was very proud of me!

But this led to a catastrophic failure. I spent all this time doing things—good things—but I didn't spend a single ounce of time developing leaders. We launched our plant in the fall of 2016 with over three-hundred people in attendance in our first service. Hundreds of people came through our doors over the next several months. When these people joined us for worship, they would often praise us for not passing an offering plate or not making visitors stand in worship to be recognized.

But we failed at the next step. They loved worship and the people they were worshiping with, but they always had the same question: How do I get connected? I had few answers. We had only a few small groups. We had very few service projects. I was working eighty hours a week and had zero time to start something else for people to get involved with. I had failed. I failed to develop and deploy leaders.

Learn from my mistakes. Make sure you are developing leaders to preach, lead small groups, manage, serve, etc.

Evaluator

How pastor-centric is your church? Consider the topics below and rate your church on how pastor-centric each topic/area is on a scale of zero (not at all pastor-centric) to ten (completely pastor-centric). What percentage of the responsibility within each area is completed by the pastor versus by a lay person?

Ministry Decisions

0   1   2   3   4   5   6   7   8   9   10

Administrative Decisions

0   1   2   3   4   5   6   7   8   9   10

Worship Planning

0   1   2   3   4   5   6   7   8   9   10

Ministry Planning

0   1   2   3   4   5   6   7   8   9   10

Building Decisions

0   1   2   3   4   5   6   7   8   9   10

Staffing Decisions

0   1   2   3   4   5   6   7   8   9   10

Discipling New People

0   1   2   3   4   5   6   7   8   9   10

Connecting with New People

0   1   2   3   4   5   6   7   8   9   10

Representing Church in Community

0   1   2   3   4   5   6   7   8   9   10

Stewardship Campaign

0   1   2   3   4   5   6   7   8   9   10

Questions

1. How has becoming pastor-centric stunted the growth of your faith community?

2. How many apostles, prophets, evangelists, shepherds, and teachers are active in your faith community? Is the full expression of God's gifts present in your congregation?

3. If your church is pastor-centric, how did your church arrive in this place? Be open and honest with one another, but this is not about blaming. It is an exercise that helps understand the root cause.

4. How are disciples formed and matured in your faith community? What is your intentional pathway of discipleship? What is the expectation of maturing as a disciple in your faith community?

5. How are laity identified, recruited, equipped, and deployed for ministry in your church? Name the intentional process and steps for accomplishing this at all age levels, discipleship maturity phases, and without being pastor-centric or staff-dependent.

CHAPTER FOUR
Moving Away from Offering-Plate Dependency

It's also like a man going off on an extended trip. He called his servants together and delegated responsibilities. To one he gave five thousand dollars, to another two thousand, to a third one thousand, depending on their abilities. Then he left. Right off, the first servant went to work and doubled his master's investment. The second did the same. But the man with the single thousand dug a hole and carefully buried his master's money.

After a long absence, the master of those three servants came back and settled up with them. The one given five thousand dollars showed him how he had doubled his investment. His master commended him: "Good work! You did your job well.

From now on, be my partner."

The servant with the two thousand showed how he also had doubled his master's investment. His master commended him: "Good work! You did your job well.

From now on, be my partner."

The servant given one thousand said, "Master, I know you have high standards and hate careless ways, that you demand the best and make no allowances for error. I was afraid I might disappoint you, so I found a good hiding place and secured your money. Here it is, safe and sound down to the last cent."

*The master was furious. "That's a terrible way to live!
It's criminal to live cautiously like that! If you knew I
was after the best, why did you do less than the least?
The least you could have done would have been to invest
the sum with the bankers, where at least I would have
gotten a little interest. Take the thousand and give it to
the one who risked the most. And get rid of this 'play-it-
safe' who won't go out on a limb. Throw him out into utter
darkness."*

Matthew 25:14-30 (MSG)

It may or may not be obvious to you, however, according to the stats church giving and tithing is on the decline. One of the most shocking statistics about church giving is that church members are currently giving a smaller percent of their income today (2.5%) than church members during the Great Depression (3.3%).

Between 1990 and 2015 the share of overall donations going to faith dropped by 50 percent (New York Times). And for the first time ever, faith giving fell below 30 percent of the total donations in Giving USA's study.[26]

In our experience, church attenders often have misguided notions about the church's income as it relates to the offering plate. To gain some perspective on the offering plate at the local church level, here are some interesting statistics:[27]

- 49 percent of all church giving transactions are made with a card.

---

[26] https://agapeinvests.com/surprising-statistics-about-tithing-and-church-giving/.

[27] https://nonprofitssource.com/online-giving-statistics/church-giving/.

- 8/10 people who give to churches have zero credit debt.

- 60% are willing to give to their church digitally.

- Tithers make up only 10-25 percent of a normal congregation.

- Churches that accept tithing online increase overall donations by 32%.

- Only 5% tithe, and 80% of Americans only give 2% of their income.

- Only 3-5% of Americans who give to their local church do so through regular tithing.

- When surveyed, 17% of Americans stated that they regularly tithe.

- For families making $75k+, 1% of them gave at least 10% in tithing.

- 3 out of 4 people who don't go to church make donations to nonprofit organizations.

- The average giving by adults who attend US Protestant churches is about $17 a week.

- 37% of regular church attendees and Evangelicals don't give money to church.

- 17% of American families have reduced the amount that they give to their local church.

- 7% of church goers have dropped regular giving by 20% or more.

- About 10 million tithers in the US donate $50 billion yearly to churches & non-profits.

Pandemic Effects on the Church

The pandemic has also affected the offering plate income. According to CapinCrouse,[28] 25 percent of churches saw no effect, while 19 percent saw an increase. However, the vast majority, 56 percent, saw a decrease in giving due to the pandemic. While COVID-19 has been a horrific pandemic that has taken over a million lives in the United States, it did not cause the majority of these issues in the Western church. The pandemic only emphasized and accelerated what was already happening. The acceleration caused the church to finally have to pay attention and stop denying the realities facing the church.

Prior to the pandemic, many smaller churches did not have an option for online giving. Some churches quickly pivoted to provide this service while others struggled to do so but eventually got there. With irregular church attendance even before the pandemic, the churches with automated giving had much more consistent giving than those without such systems.

Without automated giving options, church members, by and large, don't give when they don't attend nor do they make up those payments when they attend next. Some denominations stepped in during the pandemic and helped smaller churches get set up to take online payments, greatly benefiting those who were open to this option.

---

[28] https://www.capincrouse.com/wp-content/uploads/2020/04/CapinCrouse-2020-Impact-of-COVID-19-on-Church-Giving.pdf.

Attendance in churches was already in a tailspin pre-COVID, but for some churches, it was—or soon will be—the end of the road. In my (Kay's) consulting work, the healthiest churches grew during the pandemic due to their quick innovations and excellent online ministries. Others who were fairly healthy pre-pandemic are back at 80 to 90 percent of their pre-pandemic numbers. The vast majority of churches, however, are about 50 percent of their pre-pandemic numbers (at two years since the onset of the pandemic). You can study all kinds of general statistics and ranges of information, but it is most important for you to research the stats of your own faith community.

In the past decade of church consulting, I (Kay) have noted a growing increase in church apathy and a decrease in capacity. While there has been a presence of church leaders with a desire and heart to do whatever it might take to reach new people, there was simply not the capacity to do so. With the average age of most congregations nearing seventy years old, the energy and physical ability needed were not available. In other congregations, there has been a profound sense of apathy. Their drive and desire to reach new people left the building years ago, and they have simply been waiting for the last person to turn out the lights on their way out.

The bottom line is that the church as we have known it no longer exists. If nothing else, the pandemic gave us the opportunity and flexibility to reimagine a faith community for today's postmodern, post-Christian culture—if we are bold and courageous enough to step out in faith and make counter cultural changes in the church world to reach new people.

Shifting Culture

While the United States was once much more church-centric, that paradigm has shifted dramatically over the past decade. In fact, 2021 was the first time the percentage of people claiming membership in a church, mosque, or synagogue fell less than the majority at 47 percent. The Gallup Poll first started tracking this information in 1937 when the number was reported at 73 percent and remained above 70 percent until 2000. Between 2000 and 2020, that number sharply declined from 70 percent to 47 percent.[29]

Looking more closely at these statistics and the dramatic decline in the past fifteen years:

Three-Year Span	Percentage of Churched
1998-2000	69%
2008-2010	62%
2018-2020	49%

Some people may reason that the membership decline in local churches is attributed to the death of the Silent

---

[29] https://news.gallup.com/poll/341963/church-membership-falls-below-majority-first-time.aspx.

Generation and older members of the Boomer Generation since the average age in most churches is near seventy. However, this number is not at all reflective of the average age of thirty-eight in the US overall.

Instead, Gallup attributes the decline in church membership to the growing number of people who report no religious preference. With fewer people not affiliating with any church, there will, of course, be fewer giving units in the church to fill the offering plate. A 2020 study conducted by Faith Communities Today reported that the average church attendance had dropped from 137 in 2000 to sixty-five in 2020.[30]

Besides fewer people affiliating and attending churches, there has been a generational shift in priorities as seen in spending habits and budget allocation. For example, "Millennials crave more experiences: Not shockingly, more than 8 in 10 millennials (82%) attended or participated in a variety of live experiences in the past year, ranging from parties, concerts, festivals, performing arts and races and themed sports—and more so than other older generations (70%)."[31]

Yet, these younger generations also carry a great deal of debt. The average student loan debt is nearly $40,000, with an average repayment period lasting between eighteen and twenty-one years. They have, on average, about $20,000 in auto loans, over $4,000 in credit card debt,

---

[30] https://faithcommunitiestoday.org/fact-2020-survey/.

[31] https://eventbrite-s3.s3.amazonaws.com › marketing.

and more than $12,000 in personal loans. Generation Z is on track to have even higher debt. Add the rising cost of housing and childcare to the growing list of expenses, and these two younger adult generations are doing all they can to keep their head above water.

Though the church desires to reach Millennials and Gen Z, the church will obviously need other forms of income. These generations will not be able to support the rising costs of keeping a church on a financially healthy pathway on their own. And remember, the older generation right ahead of the Millennials is Gen X. Generation X is one of the smallest generations and is becoming increasingly less churched each year. Gen X'ers are likely to carry credit card debt and account for a much less significant percentage of the wealth (29%) than the older Boomer Generation (51%).[32]

Rising Facility Cost

Churches are feeling the pinch on their budgets from the rising costs associated with maintaining their facilities. Commercial insurance has seen increases of 8-10 percent each year for the past few years. Utilities costs are also rising. On average, electricity rates rise about 2 percent each year. For those churches with large facilities, this increase can be a significant hit. Add in the cost of normal maintenance, and the pinch on a church budget is really felt.

---

[32] https://www.investopedia.com/terms/g/generation-x-genx.asp.

Some churches utilize volunteers from the congregation to help with small maintenance jobs. These consist of duties such as changing light bulbs, landscaping, lawn maintenance, small plumbing chores, painting, mowing, cleaning, etc. Yet, in smaller churches, congregants are aging and can no longer perform some of the day-to-day maintenance they once did. This maintenance is now having to be outsourced, or the building begins to fall into a state of disrepair.

As church buildings age across the country, they are requiring more and more dollars to maintain. The outdated systems that have been duct-taped and WD-40'ed for a decade or two are now on their last leg. Parts for repairs are becoming more difficult to source. Maintenance is often delayed—sometimes for years and years. Some churches are one boiler breakdown or final roof leak away from closing. Rather than turning the building over to a congregation that can care for it (gifting to the next generation) and rather than reaching new people while the building is still in relatively good shape, the congregation too often stays open until they run out of money and the building is almost worthless because of years—if not decades—of delayed maintenance. We often wonder about the justification in both the congregation's and the judicatory leadership processes in allowing such waste and ignoring accountability of faithful stewardship.

Make an honest assessment of your facilities and grounds. Can you truly care for them in a way that honors God? Are you able to keep up with repairs and preventative maintenance? Is the facility updated regularly? Would a seeker be comfortable in the space? Ask an unchurched person to walk through your building and provide a no-holds-barred assessment of your space. Is your building the right size for your congregation? Has your congregation declined to the point of really being a small group? Hold the mirror up and take in the realistic reflection. If you need a process to help guide you through this process, check out the *Small Church Checkup* by Kotan and Schroeder.

Rising Staffing Cost

To attract and retain effective personnel, it will take more staffing dollars than it did just a year or two ago. With unemployment numbers low and minimum wage increasing, finding quality, affordable employees is becoming more difficult.

The average United Methodist full-time clergy compensation in 2021 was $74,199.[33] Add in the pension, health insurance, allowed reimbursed expenses (travel, continuing education, miscellaneous reimbursables such as computers, etc.), and housing (values of parsonage or housing allowance), and the total package is usually well over $100,000. This package is becoming increasingly more difficult for the average size church of sixty-five people to support.

---

[33] https://nccumc.org/treasurer/files/Compensation-and-Personnel-Policies-for-Pastors-2021.pdf.

Some annual conferences or other denominational judicatories require churches to have parsonages for pastors. Other annual conferences leave it up to the church to provide either a parsonage or a housing allowance. There are minimum requirements for these parsonages that must be met for access and layout. With a variety of family scenarios and abilities that could present for each new appointment, the church is liable to keep the parsonage in a good state of repair and up to parsonage standards. This requirement is yet another ongoing and increasing expense for the church.

While there is no ongoing maintenance when it comes to a housing allowance, the church is not building up any equity in real estate. There will be a constant, ongoing outlay of dollars for housing. In addition, the housing costs will continue to increase as the local housing costs increase.

Just like the increasing costs associated with clergy compensation, the same is true for staffing costs. As churches have become more staff-dependent, churches now average using 50 percent of their budget for salaries. In addition, our country continues to experience the Great Resignation, where millions are leaving their jobs monthly looking for more meaningful, flexible work that allows more time with their families. Where the church has notoriously paid lower than other sectors, people are not as likely to seek employment with the church when the trust in religious institutions is at an all-time low. And let's be honest, church employees can likely go work at the local fast-food restaurant and make as much money—or more—without the stressors they face at the church. It will take more money to attract and retain quality employees than ever before.

Story

When we started our second church in Blue Springs, we set out to do something new. So, I (Michael) spent a year interviewing church planters, reading church-planting books, and attending conferences about church planting. I wanted to learn the latest and greatest ways to plant a church. In 2015, we saw a trend developing in the Midwest of churches not passing offering plates during worship. This omittance was heretical to many churches and pastors. One pastor, a mentor and friend to me, said that any church that did that would not make it as a church. I respect this pastor, and so when we launched our new church, we created a worship service with a time of offering built into it.

A month into the launch, our worship leader and I were at a conference in a nearby town. They were talking about this idea of not passing an offering plate during worship. The megachurch we met in had offering boxes in the back of their worship space for tithes and offerings. This, along with an option for electronic giving, was their approach to generosity. My worship leader looked at me and said, "You know it's the right thing to do." She was right.

The overwhelming majority of young people believe

the church exists to take your money. We were starting something new, and if we wanted to reach the next generation, we had to do things differently. And in this case, it meant not passing an offering plate. This TERRIFIED me. How will we get money? Will people just stop giving? Will my friend's prediction come true? Will we end up closing? All these fears were simply unfounded. Now, when we ask people why they came and stayed in our church, the number one or two answer is usually "because you don't pass an offering plate." We knew we had to change this practice to reach new people, but the question remained: how would we fund our ministry? We will dig into this in Chapter 6, where we will talk about moving towards Christian social entrepreneurship.

Evaluator

How offering-plate dependent is your church? Consider the topics below and rate your church on how offering-plate dependent it is in each topic/area on a scale of zero (not at all offering-plate dependent—meaning tithes, offerings, fundraisers) to ten (completely offering-plate dependent for all expenses).

Worship Expenses

0   1   2   3   4   5   6   7   8   9   10

Building Debt

0   1   2   3   4   5   6   7   8   9   10

Building Maintenance/Overhead Expenses

0   1   2   3   4   5   6   7   8   9   10

Capital Improvements

0   1   2   3   4   5   6   7   8   9   10

Personnel Expenses

0   1   2   3   4   5   6   7   8   9   10

Leadership Development

0   1   2   3   4   5   6   7   8   9   10

All Ministry Expenditures

0   1   2   3   4   5   6   7   8   9   10

Evangelism/Outreach

0　1　2　3　4　5　6　7　8　9　10

Innovation/New Ministries

0　1　2　3　4　5　6　7　8　9　10

Denominational Fees

0　1　2　3　4　5　6　7　8　9　10

Questions

1. Look at your church's expenses and income from the offering plate over the past five years. How much is the church really investing in the mission of making disciples versus paying salaries and maintaining facilities?

2. What areas of ministry is the church funding fully, and what areas are underfunded? How much is each area underfunded? What is the total amount of underfunding?

3. How effective is the offering plate for creating the needed income to accomplish the true ministry needed in your mission field to reach the new people God is calling you to reach?

4. How open are your leaders to really considering other options beyond the offering plate to fund ministry? How open are your congregation members to other options?

5. Some expenses are fixed, and only so many cutbacks are possible before there are no more options to cut. How close is your church to this tipping point? Who in your community is not being introduced to Jesus because other sources of income are not being considered?

CHAPTER FIVE
Becoming Emotionally & Culturally Competent

While Jesus and his disciples were traveling,
Jesus entered a village where a woman
named Martha welcomed him as a guest.
She had a sister named Mary,
who sat at the Lord's feet and listened to his message.
By contrast, Martha was preoccupied with
getting everything ready for their meal.
So Martha came to him and said,
"Lord, don't you care that my sister has left me
to prepare the table all by myself?
Tell her to help me."
The Lord answered, "Martha, Martha,
you are worried and distracted by many things.
One thing is necessary.
Mary has chosen the better part.
It won't be taken away from her."

Luke 10:38-42 (CEB)

Many churches continue to be very busy. Congregants faithfully carry on the traditional annual dinners, annual auctions, annual Lord's acres sales, annual pumpkin patches, annual Vacation Bible Schools, annual Easter egg hunts, annual trunk-or-treats, annual breakfast with

Santa, annual cantatas, annual Christmas pageants or programs, annual basement sale or clothing giveaway, annual ladies tea, annual turkey dinner, annual chili cook-off, annual sweetheart banquet, and annual ....

This busyness has continued despite the often-experienced decline in the number of people available to plan and conduct these events and programs, let alone the number of people attending. Yet, because it is a "tradition" to hold these events and programs annually, they continue.

We so often fail to evaluate the effectiveness of these ministries. What is their purpose? Who is this ministry intended to reach? Is this a ministry to build relationships with new people? Is this a ministry to disciple people? Is it serving the purpose any longer? Is the investment of time, energy, dollars, and other resources worth the outcome? How many new relationships were created through this ministry? How many people were introduced to Jesus through this ministry? How did people take their next faithful step in discipleship formation as a result of this ministry? How were lives transformed through these ministries by those participating? What ripple effects do these ministries have on individuals, the church, and the community?

Ministries are methods.
Ministries are not traditions.

Ministries are the delivery methods used to accomplish the mission of making disciples, the purpose the church exists. When a ministry becomes a tradition (second annual, fifth annual, twentieth annual), it no longer is a tool for discipleship. It has instead become more about nostalgia, expectation, and/or heritage. Why do we hold this event every year? Because we've "always done it this way."

I (Kay) have worked with churches that have come to the realization a particular ministry needs to stop, but they haven't been willing to pull the plug, celebrate its life, and give it a funeral. Why? Because Aunt Ethyl started that ministry forty years ago, and no one wants to hurt Aunt Ethyl's feelings by no longer hosting the annual fried chicken dinner over the Fourth of July. Tradition! Personal preferences over missional alignment and accountability.

Who's Our Neighbor?

As a congregation sinks further into tradition and nostalgia, it also often pulls further away from its neighbors. In the busyness of keeping up with the calendar of annual expectations, a congregation can become so focused on those who are already gathered within the faith community that they lose touch with those in the community that Jesus commissions them to reach.

Go out and make disciples in all the nations.
Ceremonially wash them through baptism
in the name of the triune God:
Father, Son, and Holy Spirit.

*Then disciple them. Form them in the practices and
postures that I have taught you, and show them how to
follow the commands I have laid down for you.*
*And I will be with you, day after day,
to the end of the age.*

Matthew 28:19-20 (VOICE)

There is more than one way to lose touch with people.
First, congregations lose touch by not knowing who their
neighbors are. Second, not only do they not know their
neighbors' names, but they also don't know their stories,
their concerns, their worries, their fears, how they spend
their time, what they enjoy doing, what kind of work they
do, and so on. Third, congregations have lost touch with
how they might even build a bridge to reach their neighbors
and how to build relationships with them. Out-of-touch
congregations have lost their cultural competence.

The majority of churches are in decline. An estimated
30 percent are dying, 35 percent are not thriving and
struggling, 25 percent are not thriving but could, and only
10 percent of American churches are thriving. Did you
catch that? Let me repeat, only 10 percent of American
churches are thriving at this time. Why is this? We believe
that churches have not been focused or intentional in living
out their purpose. Unfortunately, too many churches have
instead slipped into being a social club that caters to the
desires and preferences of their members and does some
occasional charity work. With this country-club approach
focused on providing benefits and services for its members,
the church has become culturally or emotionally

incompetent to function effectively in the post-Christian, postmodern world we live in.

Most churches function as though we continue to live in a church-centric culture. In other words, they still operate like the majority of the population in today's American culture has the natural tendency, desire, and moral compass to be drawn or attracted to a church or religion. Congregations with this misguided belief might state these types of explanations for the decline at their church council meetings:

- If we just had the right young pastor with three kids appointed here, we would be just fine. This is an appointment problem.

  Hint: Your church probably would not like the things the young pastor would suggest the church needed to do or change to reach others like the pastor's family.

- If we just had a bigger building, people would be rushing in the doors. This is a facility issue.

  Hint: If this strategy really worked, the majority of churches would not be in decline. There is way too much empty church real estate for anyone to still believe this myth.

- If we just launched a new ministry or a ministry like the church down the street where "everybody in town" is going, people would flock to the church. This is a programming dilemma.

  Hint: New ministries are not magnets that automatically draw people to churches. Ministries are planned strategically with a specific group of people in mind to accomplish a specific purpose.

- If we just had more money, we would have no worries, and we would be able to do effective ministry to reach all the people we could handle. This is a financial issue.

  Hint: The most effective ministry any church could engage in costs no money at all: building relationships with your neighbors. Building relationships costs zero dollars. Some of the wealthiest churches are dying.

- If we could just hire a good youth director, we could have young families back in the church. This is a staffing problem.

  Hint: A church can't thrive based on one person carrying the load. Furthermore, a thriving church doesn't hire staff to do the ministry for them.

☙

Let's be honest: Religion has probably never had such a bad name. Christianity is now seen as "irrelevant" by some, "toxic" by many, and often as a large part of the problem rather than any kind of solution. Some of us are almost embarrassed to say we are Christian because of the negative images that word conjures in others' minds. Young people especially are turned off by how judgmental, exclusionary, impractical, and ineffective Christian culture seems to be.

We must rediscover what St. Francis of Assisi (1182–1226) called the "marrow of the Gospel." It's time to rebuild from the bottom up. If the foundation is not solid and sure, everything we try to build on top of it is weak and ineffective. Perhaps it's a blessing in disguise that so much is tumbling down around us. It's time to begin again. In the year 1205, Jesus spoke to Francis through the San Damiano cross: "Francis, rebuild my church, for you see it is falling into ruin."

If Jesus himself says the church is falling into ruin, I guess we can admit it also without being accused of being negative or unbelieving. Maybe we have to admit it for anything new and good to happen.

Richard Rohr
Daily Meditations

Developing Cultural and Emotional Competency

In his book, *Cultural Competency: Partnering With Your Neighbors in Your Ministry Expedition,* Paul Nixon offers us a very helpful list that he refers to as baselines that transcend culture. He explains using these baselines to build cultural competency like this: "The Gospel of Jesus provides a serious baseline for us in all that we do. Any principle related to the work of ministering across cultures, that is truly a baseline, would have to always be true." It was with that in mind that Paul offered the following cultural competency baselines:

- The Christian Good News transcends culture.

- Your church belongs to God, not to you.

- The Good Ole Days are in front of us, not behind us.

- Authenticity is essential – don't try to be something (or somebody) that you are not.

- No church can serve everybody – so each church had better get focused on particular "somebodies."

- Friendship first, then ministry development.

- Cultural competency requires spiritual readiness.

- Social privilege often gets in our way.

- Community partnerships are priceless.

- Good listening may lead to un-learning, which leads to even better listening.

- A lot of what we try will go about as well as a Wile E. Coyote scheme.

- God is alive and at work in every neighborhood – our challenge is to show up to what God is doing.

- Regardless of strategy, spiritual collaboration with new people is essential.

Take time to ponder the list above by yourself. You might even journal about each point. Which ones are you struggling with as a baseline truth? Why might this be the case? Spend some time in prayer. Next, dialogue with other leaders in your church about the list. Which baselines might be getting in the way of the church's mission of reaching new people? How open are the leaders to helping the congregation become more culturally and emotionally competent so they can be faithful to carry out the Great Commission given to the church by Jesus? What are some first steps to take to learn and what can be done? Who might be helpful (collaborative partners, mentors) in this learning process?

What exactly is cultural competency (aka cultural intelligence or CQ)? According to dictionary.com, *cultural competence* is "the ability to effectively interact with people from cultures different from one's own, especially through knowledge and appreciation of cultural differences. In general, competence means possessing the necessary skill or knowledge to handle a particular situation or task." Cultural competence is the ability to examine the various social and cultural identities, understand and appreciate diversity, recognize and respond to cultural demands and opportunities as well as build relationships across cultural backgrounds.

Similarly, according to Wikipedia, *emotional competence* (aka emotional intelligence or EQ) "refers to an important set of personal and social skills for identifying, interpreting, and constructively responding to emotions in oneself and others." It includes self-awareness, self-management, social awareness, and relationship management. The term implies ease in getting along with others and determines one's ability to lead and express oneself effectively and successfully. Psychologists define emotional competence as the ability to monitor one's own and others' feelings and emotions and use this information to guide one's thinking and actions. It is also often referred to as emotional intelligence.

At its very basic level, EQ describes a high level of self and social awareness and management, while CQ describes a high level of awareness and appreciation for diversity. With both EQ and CQ, building relationships with people who are different from ourselves is much easier—or at least less challenging. In fact, some people live to meet new people. They thrive on interacting with diverse people, hearing their interesting new stories, and learning new things.

According to Syracuse University, cultural competence encompasses:[34]

- **being aware** of one's own worldview

- **developing positive attitudes** towards cultural differences

- **gaining knowledge** of different cultural practices and world views

- **developing skills** for communication and interaction across cultures

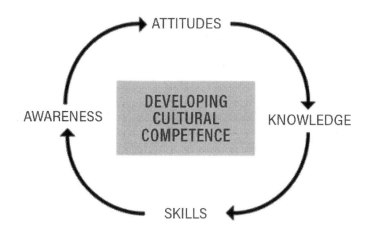

34   https://researchguides.library.syr.edu/fys101/cultural_compentence.

Becoming and staying culturally and emotionally competent is an ongoing process. Just like leadership is an ongoing process, CQ and EQ require us to continuously learn and grow. While some of these skills develop from education, a great deal of this competency is developed through immersing oneself in different cultures and circumstances. We are not suggesting that you need to hop on a plane to another country. A different culture is likely across the street or around the corner. Take a look at the illustration below of the "Cultural Iceberg."

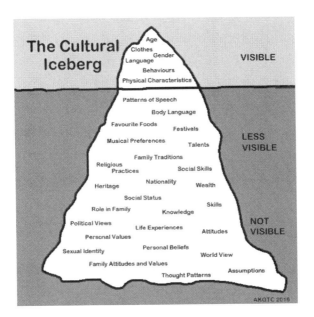

When we consider cultural differences, we likely immediately think about those characteristics that appear above the water level in the illustration above. We might think about those just under the water level. But notice that the majority of the cultural differences are not just below the surface, but deep below the surface and not even visible to most people. In other words, we do not see these differences and, therefore, do not even think about them— at least initially.

Yet, in the life of the church, because we don't see or think about all these differences, we have a hard time understanding why "they" (aka our neighbors yet to be gathered) don't flock to our church, like what we like, and do what we do. This is where CQ (our empathy, openness, and desire to build relationships with people different from ourselves) and EQ (having self and social awareness of how we show up in relationships with others and a desire to build relationships with others) are essential when we begin to step outside our church buildings and begin building relationships with our neighbors. Without CQ and EQ, we may do more harm than good. Part of CQ and EQ is intertwined with being a mature disciple in that it calls for us to look beyond ourselves, beyond our wants and needs. We are no longer the primary focus.

> *It is good for those who have had the dominant culture position to learn with an attitude of humility and to acknowledge that our dominant posture has often made us arrogant, complacent, entitled, and proud.*[35]
>
> **Jon Tyson and Heather Grizzle**

Instead of being bound by what Mom might have taught us, "treat others like you want to be treated," maybe we instead need to approach meeting our new

---

[35] Tyson and Grizzle, *A Creative Minority,* Grizzle Publishing, 2016.

neighbors with a renewed sense of love expressed as, "treat others as they would like to be treated."

So now what?

We who are strong are not just to satisfy our own desires. We are called to carry the weaknesses of those who are not strong.

Each of us must strive to please our neighbors, pursuing their welfare so they will become strong.

The Anointed One Himself is our model for this kind of living, for He did not live to please Himself.

And as the Scriptures declared, "When they insult You, they insult me."

Romans 15:1-3 (VOICE)

In Romans 15, Paul gives us a lesson in CQ:

Paul says he is free to eat, but he is not free to injure another in what he eats. Personal freedom must always give way to corporate responsibility. To put it another way, the gospel of love demands that we surrender individual liberties for the sake of our brothers and sisters. We see this demonstrated powerfully in the example of Jesus, who gave up His life and freedom for the sake of the world. When we live by this ethic (CQ, EQ, mature disciple), we create a community marked by warmth and hospitality…But justice, peace, and joy are communal essentials for life in the Kingdom.[36]

---

[36] https://www.biblegateway.com, Romans 15, *The Voice.*

"The Cosmic Egg" offers yet another tool to help us understand cultural and emotional intelligence. This concept was originally attributed to Joseph Chilton Pearce (1926-2016), but most recently is used in Richard Rohr's book, *The Wisdom Pattern: Order, Disorder, Reorder.* This diagram offers further insight into developing cultural and emotional competency. Notice that the innermost circle, or dome, is focused on self and is referenced as "My Story." While we must have keen self-awareness of who we are, we can't stop with ourselves being the center of the universe.

The next dome encompasses both self and groups. This layer includes groupings such as family, ethnicity, gender, religion, and occupation. Rohr calls this "Our Story" and says this is where most people in all of human history have lived their lives.

The third and largest dome is referred to as "The Story." This outermost dome encompasses "My Story," "Our Story," and "The Story." As Rohr explains:

> The Story refers to "the patterns that are always true—beyond anecdote and my cultural history. Biblical revelation says that the only way we can move to The Story and understand it with any depth is to walk through and take responsibility for both our personal story and our group story. Anything less we now call "spiritual bypassing." When all three domes of meaning are deemed worthy of love and attention, we probably have a rather mature spiritual person.[37]

---

[37] https://cac.org/daily-meditations/the-three-domes-2021-01-24/.

The Cosmic Egg

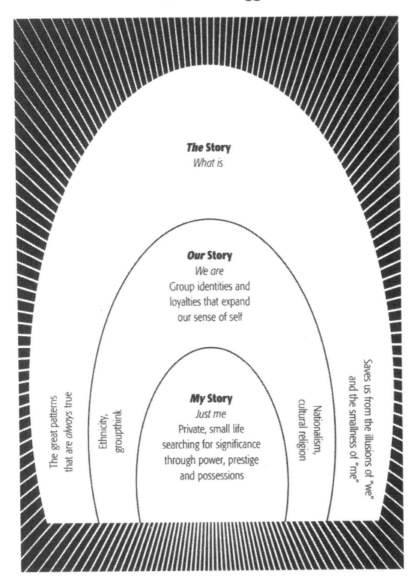

Healthy and biblical religion
includes the whole cosmic egg.

Defining, Naming, and Claiming Your Neighborhood

How would you define your church's community? Yes, it includes the people already gathered as part of the congregation, but our primary focus must be those yet-to-be gathered. Who specifically are these yet-to-be-gathered people your church needs to focus on reaching? Yes, the world is your parish; however, look back at the fifth baseline on Nixon's list. No one church can be all things to all people. Your church was planted in your particular neighborhood to reach that neighborhood. As long as your church is sitting in that location, your church has an obligation and a responsibility to reach these neighbors for Jesus. If your church is unwilling or unable to do so, it is time to turn the keys over to those who are willing and able. The world needs Jesus too much for any church to ignore that the Great Commission needs to start within its own neighborhood.

It is important to specifically define your neighborhood, aka mission field. Your neighborhood includes the immediate area surrounding the church facility. For smaller communities and rural areas, the neighborhood is likely the entire town. For more densely populated areas, it could be just a few blocks. Typically, the area you want to identify has a population under ten thousand. It is the area in which people of the area typically live, shop, eat, and where the children go to school, etc. Sometimes natural transitions exist between neighborhoods where people can sense they are moving from one area to the next. It is helpful to identify these natural boundaries.

The mission field can be defined by indicators such as a radius around your church location, a zip code, parameters of a school district, or by a particular road or landmark in each direction (i.e., Maple Street to the north, the railroad tracks to the south, 20th Street to the west, and Lazy River to the east).

Church leaders must not take this exercise lightly or consider it an exercise in futility. This is not only important work, but this is also holy work. Do prayer walks through the neighborhood. Who is God calling you to reach? Spend some time in discernment. This work will not be accomplished in one meeting at a table looking at a map. This research enables you to specifically identify where your congregation will invest in new relationships, get to know people inextricably, and journey with them in their faith walk.

First, name your mission field (boundaries). Claim your mission field (God is calling us to reach the people living here). Third, take responsibility for reaching your neighbors (take intentional steps to invest relationally with cultural and emotional competence).

Start on Paper and Understanding Change Management

What percentage of your congregation lives in the neighborhood? After reviewing demographics reports, how does your congregation reflect the neighborhood? In other words, is the primary *Mosaic group* or segment or two in the neighborhood also present in the congregation? Are the preferences of those already gathered and the largest population demographic in the neighborhood aligned?

If you are unfamiliar with these terms, it will be important for you to familiarize yourself with them. This will help with narrowing the cultural competence gap. *Mosaic USA* was developed by Experian, which classifies households in the United States into nineteen groups and subdivides them further into seventy-one unique segments that share similar demographic and socioeconomic characteristics. These profiles provide information about lifestyles, behaviors, affluence, life stage, ethnicity, housing, income, household size, and much more.

The MissionImpact Guide goes into further detail, providing preferences for each segment in the areas of communication, leadership, small group, finances, worship, facilities, education, outreach, and hospitality.

Many churches use MissionInsite for demographic information and reports. Besides general demographic information, the MissionImpact Guide can be found on their website along with other resources:

https://help.acst.com/en/missioninsite/guides/the-missionimpact-guide

If your church leaders do not have any experience walking through demographic reports, pulling out the important information, and interpreting it properly, it might be helpful to call in some assistance from a coach or consultant who has experience doing this kind of work with congregations.

After naming, claiming, and taking responsibility for your mission field and after taking in all the demographic information, the next step is to determine your targeted demographic. Which Mosaic segment does your congregation feel it is most equipped, ready, and willing to reach? Again, this is not a decision to make without prayer and discernment. Likely, changes will need to be made. For there to be enough time, energy, and passion to reach the neighbors, some beloved ministries may need to be set aside. Some dollars in the budget may need to be shuffled away from traditional ministries to new ones that will more likely reach the neighbors. Some of the attention on the already-gathered congregation may need to be shifted to reach the neighbors.

In leading such a transition (change management), it is important to increase congregational care. Notice the word *congregational* and not *pastoral*. Those already gathered will need to provide most of the care for those already gathered so that the pastor and other leaders can identify, recruit, equip, and deploy disciples into the community to build relationships with the neighbors. The pastor will need to be present for critical-care situations, but routine care needs to transition to congregational care after proper training and communication.

One more important reminder about leading change.

Always start with the *why,* not the *what.* Telling the congregation that the pastor and leaders don't have time to visit the shut-ins anymore so someone else will be visiting because those leaders are now spending their time with new people will not be helpful. Instead, it would be more helpful if the messaging is something like this: "As followers of Jesus, we are called to love our neighbors and teach them the ways of Jesus. We will live that out by caring for one another through congregational care and by going out and building new relationships with our neighbors in more intentional ways in the coming weeks and months."

Becoming *OF* the Community

You already know how exhausting, uncreative, and unsatisfying it is to reduce innovation to modes of acquisition (i.e. getting more butts, buildings, and budgets). You may have already begun to wonder what it looks like when Christian communities flourish not because they are strategic or even potentially successful, but because they add sacred value to human life.[38]

Kenda Creasy Dean

To bring sacred value to human life, we must become "of" the community. The church and its already-gathered individuals must actively participate in the community and immerse themselves into the mission field (do "life"

---

[38] Kenda Creasy Dean, *Innovating for Love: Joining God's Expedition through Christian Social Innovation,* Market Square Publishing, 2022.

in the neighborhood). This pertains to both individuals in the congregations and the church overall. This is more difficult for churches when most of their already-gathered congregants drive into the mission field from afar. Yet this circumstance does not eliminate the responsibility and obligation to be involved in the life of the surrounding community. When a person becomes part of a faith community, they become a vital part of living out the mission and vision of that faith community.

The church must be able to calculate a measurable impact occurring in the neighborhood because the church exists. The people's lives in the neighborhood should be better because of the church and its ministries. In other words, if the church were to close tomorrow, it would be greatly missed because the impact on the community is so deep and wide. To have this kind of impact on the neighborhood, the church will need to have its finger on the pulse of the community, monitoring any changes and adjusting as necessary to stay competent, compelling, and relevant. As demographics, needs, or gaps change, the church would pivot and respond accordingly.

For church disciples, this means they are immersed in the community. They live in the community. They live, shop, eat, walk, bike, and network in the neighborhood. They intentionally place themselves in situations to meet new people in the neighborhood. They are curious about people's journeys and open to learning their stories. They build new relationships with people who are different from themselves. Through the immersion into the mission field and openness to these new relationships through the lens of CQ and EQ, they can better understand how the church might be helpful to the neighbors, have a deeper impact on the neighborhood, and over time, might develop a relationship with enough trust to be able to share their faith.

This approach turns our customary 21st-century approach to church life upside down. It is a call to evert the church and our lives, expose ourselves to different people and become more aware and more emotionally and culturally competent. In the process of "exposing" ourselves and everting the church, we must humble ourselves and become more vulnerable. We are literally turning ourselves inside out. Instead of expecting our unchurched neighbors—now the majority population—to come to the church doused in its traditional churched culture, we challenge the church to become competent and willing to go out and engage the unchurched culture with love.

Paul Nixon challenges us once again from his book, *Cultural Competency: Partnering with Your Neighbors in Your Ministry Expedition.*[39]

> *Every church can do work to get more prepared for the ministry God calls it to! We sometimes have to learn new languages, requiring hours of study. We have to get*

---

[39] Paul Nixon, *Cultural Competency: Partnering with Your Neighbors in Your Ministry Expedition,* Market Square Publishing, 2020.

out into the community, requiring hours of listening and partnering. We have to examine our social and racial privilege in terms of how it blinds us to ourselves and sabotages any Good News that we seek to advance in the world. But finally, cultural competency is a Gift of the Spirit.

It starts with just one conversation. Be curious. Be open. Be humble. Be vulnerable. Lead with love. Approach each interaction through the lens of God's love.

> *It is clear to me now that God plays no favorites, that God accepts every person whatever his or her culture or ethnic background, that God welcomes all who revere Him and do right.*
>
> **Acts 10:34-35 (VOICE)**

Story

Several years ago, I (Michael) was talking with a pastor friend of mine. This pastor had moved several times in the last few years due to conflicts in the communities and was struggling again in their current appointment. We were talking about things they had done at other churches before and things they were trying to do at their current church. (By the way, this person is an APE like we discussed in Chapter 3. This person is an entrepreneur through and through). The pastor talked about how they had achieved several successful projects throughout the last few years and how they couldn't understand why the people around them kept having issues with their approach to ministry. The pastor said to me, "I have dreams and ideas that I want to accomplish." After they said that, I asked them to pause and say it again: You have dreams and ideas? As one of their leaders, what if you thought of your role as helping (equipping & training) them to live out their dreams and ideas instead of trying to sell them on your dreams and ideas?

Our neighbors sometimes push back on "our" ideas as leaders because our ideas often reflect who we are and not the community around us. I believe engaging with the community is the best way to become culturally relevant in your mission field—especially if you are newer to the area, but this also applies to tenured pastors. Assisting people in the community who already know their neighborhoods and context to do ministry where they are will help your church become culturally relevant.

Evaluator

How culturally and emotionally competent is your church? Consider the topics below and rate your church on how culturally and emotionally competent it is in each topic/area on a scale of zero (not at all culturally and emotionally competent) to ten (totally culturally and emotionally competent).

Worship

0   1   2   3   4   5   6   7   8   9   10

Ministries

0 1 2 3 4 5 6 7 8 9 10

Paid Staff

0 1 2 3 4 5 6 7 8 9 10

Leadership Board/Council

0 1 2 3 4 5 6 7 8 9 10

Discipleship

0 1 2 3 4 5 6 7 8 9 10

Evangelism

0 1 2 3 4 5 6 7 8 9 10

Hospitality

0 1 2 3 4 5 6 7 8 9 10

Connection

0 1 2 3 4 5 6 7 8 9 10

Missions/Service

0 1 2 3 4 5 6 7 8 9 10

Overall Congregation

0 1 2 3 4 5 6 7 8 9 10

Questions

1. As an individual, what specifically did you learn from this chapter? What has challenged you the most? How did it challenge you? Why do you think it challenged you?

2. Gather as leaders and share your answers to the first question. What did you learn from one another? Did you find any common threads? How did this conversation with one another inform the next steps that need to be taken as a church?

3. As you gather your demographic information and study the demographic reports, what are you learning? What is surprising? How does what you are learning help inform new steps forward that might be more effective in reaching your neighbors?

4. As leaders, what changes might you need to navigate in order to faithfully live out the Great Commission? How difficult will these changes be for your congregation? Why will these changes be difficult for your congregation?

5. What training or resources might need to be brought in to help your congregation become more CQ & EQ?

CHAPTER SIX
Moving Towards Christian Social Entrepreneurship

When Jesus arrived and saw a large crowd, he had compassion for them and healed those who were sick. That evening his disciples came and said to him, "This is an isolated place and it's getting late. Send the crowds away so they can go into the villages and buy food for themselves."

But Jesus said to them, "There's no need to send them away. You give them something to eat."

They replied, "We have nothing here except five loaves of bread and two fish."

He said, "Bring them here to me." He ordered the crowds to sit down on the grass. He took the five loaves of bread and the two fish, looked up to heaven, blessed them and broke the loaves apart and gave them to his disciples.

Then the disciples gave them to the crowds. Everyone ate until they were full, and they filled twelve baskets with the leftovers. About five thousand men plus women and children had eaten.

Matthew 14:14-21 (CEB)

What is a social entrepreneur?

A social entrepreneur is a person who establishes an organization to solve an issue or problem or to bring about a positive change for a group of people or community. A Christian social entrepreneur is a person who establishes an organization to solve an issue or a problem or to bring about a positive change for a group of people or a community because of their love of Jesus and a desire for others to know the same love. It is a both/and approach. It is entrepreneurship for the sake of both positive social impact and fruitful Kingdom impact.

We suggest that a spiritual community who becomes "successful" (measured by community and Kingdom impact) and a social entrepreneurial organization share some common characteristics in their approaches. Here is a sampling of those healthy and effective approaches.

1. First and foremost, a congregation must have a big heart for its community. For this to be Christian AND social entrepreneurship, it is not centered around making a profit. Christian social entrepreneurship starts because the church sees that a big part of being the church is bearing the burden for the community, making it a better place to live for the people. It also funds the ministry so that the impact can be compounded.

2. The faith community has made significant progress in shifting from its historical descriptors: a building,

116

Sunday, pastor, and offering-plate-centric. While not all four shifts need to be completed, the congregation as a whole is not stuck in all four traditional models. There is simply not enough energy for leaders to move the congregation out of these deep ruts and live into a brand-new way of being a faith community at the same time.

3. If the faith community has not yet begun to make any of the shifts to move away from being building-, Sunday-, pastor-, and offering-plate-centric, there are enough resources to handle both the traditional desires of the congregation and the innovative ministry to reach new people. This normally means there is a significant number of mature, sold-out disciples with a key staff member or two who will lead the new Christian social entrepreneurship while the existing traditional "services" provided to the traditional congregation are not disrupted. It can be done, but doing both well is much more difficult to accomplish.

   Unfortunately, churches normally wait until they are desperate before exploring this option. By this time, those mature, sold-out disciples who have the desire and passion to pursue Christian social entrepreneurship have long since left. Remember, the APEs (Apostles, Prophets, Evangelists) are the ones who typically give up trying to live out their ministry within the church and leave. They find they typically have to live out their ministry outside the church.

4. The faith communities that successfully launch Christian social entrepreneurial organizations or initiatives are the ones that are culturally and emotionally competent. They are often diverse spiritual communities that live in the neighborhood. They do life already with the very people they are trying to reach. Therefore, they do not have a large cultural and emotional gap that other congregations with that gap have to first overcome before reaching their neighborhoods. Since the members of the faith community live in the community and are involved in it, they more easily and readily identify the gaps and opportunities in the community where the church can be most helpful and have the greatest impact.

5. Faith communities that become Christian social entrepreneurs have a significant number of humble, mature disciples. These disciples have moved well beyond church being "what's in it for them" and now understand it is all about "giving away Jesus to others." These disciple-making disciples possess a strong desire to share their faith with others. In addition, they may likely have an entrepreneurial background or natural tendency and likely have a clergy leader who shares the same passion. In our experience, this often (but not always) means the pastor is either a second-career pastor or not seminary trained.

6. Christian social entrepreneurs are generally more optimistic people. Kenda Creasy Dean offers these insights:

They steward abundance rather than manage scarcity. Innovating for love requires a mindset of abundance and not scarcity. Scarcity tends to dominate modern financial thinking; the shift to an abundance mindset is as much a creative challenge as a financial one. Yet innovating for love requires an economy of abundance. God calls us to steward waterfalls, not ration drinks in a drought.[40]

Pinching pennies and leading with a scarcity mindset is not only ineffective, but it certainly does not place our best foot forward as the church. We are not representing Jesus well. On Carey Nieuwhof's 487th Leadership Podcast, Dave Ramsey made this great comment:

We're not going to walk around telling people we're Christians unless we are the best in the market because we're a bad witness for Jesus when we're substandard.[41]

A church does not wake up one day and decide to pursue Christian social entrepreneurship. The church (or leader or small group depending on context and circumstances) needs to enter into the decision to pursue Christian social entrepreneurship through prayer and discernment. Examine your motives, your commitment,

---

[40] Kenda Creasy Dean, *Innovating for Love: Joining God's Expedition through Christian Social Innovation,* Market Square Books, 2022.

[41] https://careynieuwhof.com/episode487/

your resources, and the depth and thoroughness of the information upon which your decision is being made.

Entrepreneurship is Wesleyan

As Methodists, we need to be reminded that we have been rooted in entrepreneurship from the very beginning. In *John Wesley, Compassionate Entrepreneur: A Wesleyan View of Business and Entrepreneurship* by Jay Moon, Banseok Cho, and Nickolas Bettis, these writers describe Wesley's social entrepreneurship as this:

> *He provided believers with practical guidance and theological foundations for business and entrepreneurship particularly in the context of poverty. We argue that Wesley should be viewed as a compassionate entrepreneur— with the compassion of a liberator and the practice of an entrepreneur, as he encouraged believers to actively participate in economic activities, and recognized entrepreneurship as a sustainable and significant way to empower the poor. Wesley's example challenges the church today as his case study serves as a radical and faithful application of biblical economic teachings on business and entrepreneurship.*

Methodists were once known to build and operate schools, orphanages, and hospitals because they were needed in the community, and the profits could be reinvested into the ministry. Clive Murray Norris also reminds us how Wesley started the Methodist movement by integrating the church and the marketplace. In *John*

Wesley: Prophet and Entrepreneur,[42] Norris states:

> *Wesley created social enterprises to meet the needs of the poor and sick; he established a highly profitable publishing company; he found a range of ways to encourage businessmen and businesswomen to become financial supporters of Methodism; and in some ways, his whole movement can be seen as a large and successful religious enterprise, competing in a religious marketplace.*

Wesley and his associates sought to maintain the integrity of this prophetic vision while simultaneously working closely with the beneficiaries and victims of the Industrial and Consumer Revolutions and the many social changes associated with them. Wesley was even known for adapting factories into sanctuaries in England. He didn't believe spaces needed to be expensive to hold worship services. In fact, that's probably what made him so approachable to the commoner. He was sensible and moderate in his financial values, but he was willing to take risks for the betterment of the community.

Notice that social entrepreneurship is rooted in solving a community problem, bridging a community gap, meeting a community need, or making the community a better place to live. Too often, the church has a passion for a ministry, but it is not rooted in meeting a community's need or desire. And don't forget the core foundation of innovating for love.

---

[42] Clive Norris, *Servant Leadership, Social Entrepreneurship and the Will to Serve,* pp. 373-389.

Types of Christian Social Entrepreneurship

An article entitled "5 Types of Entrepreneurships: Which One Should You Pursue?" on *fool.com* describes *social entrepreneurship:*

> *A socially conscious business is focused on solving social problems, such as access to food, money, and education. The stated goal of these companies (or organizations) is to make the world better (although, for most, the ultimate purpose is still to make money). Such companies develop products and services with the goal of achieving these lofty goals. This model sometimes describes nonprofit organizations as well.*

Often, church leaders are reluctant to pursue social entrepreneurship. Typically, the reasons are one or more of the following:

1. The church is not/should not be a "business"

2. It's against "the rules" for the church to make any profit

3. No training or understanding of social entrepreneurship

4. Never needed to think about it because the offering plate covered expenses

5. Never considered it

With the acceleration of the already declining church during COVID, the wake-up call to most leaders has now been answered out of necessity. But now some churches find themselves behind the eight ball—or at least without as much time or resources as they once had—to pursue options, all the while still struggling with some reluctance.

Another mistake churches sometimes make is that they start a ministry that their church does not have the passion or capacity to maintain, so they outsource it (i.e., daycare, preschool, food pantry). Once the church is no longer involved, the chance for "ministry" (disciple making) to occur within the social entrepreneurship becomes unlikely, and the church's mission and vision cease to exist.

An additional mistake I (Kay) see churches make is that they don't continuously evaluate and pivot as needed. Once they settle into a model, it's as though the plan is written in stone, even if it no longer meets a community need or is no longer effective or profitable. Besides the five reasons mentioned above for being reluctant, these three common mistakes must also be overcome for churches to truly be fruitful and vital as social entrepreneurs.

Imagine community tables being built through social entrepreneurship that invite people into faith conversations.

Rise of Nonprofits

Innovating for Love: Christian Social Innovation by Kenda Creasy Dean is part of *The Greatest Expedition* series, collaboration between nineteen church thought leaders from around the country. Each author and resource offers precious golden nuggets of wisdom and the next bold steps for this postmodern and post-pandemic culture the church finds itself needing to navigate. *Innovating for Love* is no exception and very timely for conversations occurring at many church council meetings.

Often, church leaders and pastors are a bit averse to the word *innovation* when it comes to the church. Criticism about innovation may come in pushback like this: "The gospel hasn't changed, so why should we change how we do church?" Or, "Innovation is about business, not about the church." I even had a young pastor scoff recently when I used the word innovation, suggesting that innovation is just the latest trend in church revitalization language. But true Christian social innovation is about adding sacred value to the lives of the people in the community the church is called to serve and share Jesus. For us, innovation goes well beyond strategic plans, a tenant in the building, or the latest buzzwords and trends. It is about loving the people in the church's mission field as Jesus taught us to love.

In *The Greatest Expedition* series book *Innovating for Love: Christian Social Innovation*, Creasy Dean describes Christian social innovation in this way (page 53):

> *The impetus for Christian social innovation is not having a great idea, maximizing productivity, or needing to survive. We innovate for love to give shape to a prophetic*

imagination and to embody a vision for human flourishing
patterned after Jesus, whose way of being human is the
template for our own.

In my (Kay's) consulting work, there is often the controversy about whether the church is or should be a business or whether a ministry or innovation can be profitable for the benefit of or reinvestment into the ministry. I think the answer is a definite YES! It is not either/or. It is both. And, our roots are founded in such history and logic. Wesley was a Christian social innovator. He created businesses that provided jobs for the poor. He launched a publishing business. When a community needed medical care, the Methodists built the hospitals. The Methodists also provided much-needed orphanages and schools.

The church needs to become a vital part of the community. When we separate the church from the community, the church becomes insular and loses relevancy and competency for reaching the people in its mission field. A church's commitment to its community is both an investment in the people and for the people because we want to love like Jesus loved.

We have observed many pastors exiting church ministry to pursue and engage in the non-religious, not-for-profit world. We have also observed this trend of gravitating to nonprofits amongst Gen Z.

I (Michael) serve in our local school district for students in an "entrepreneur" track. As part of this entrepreneur experience, we have our version of the television show "Shark Tank" where the students pitch ideas for a business. More than half of the ideas are for nonprofits, and almost all of them contain some kind of "mission" for marginalized people in the community. One idea was pitched for a company to provide second-chance jobs to people who have been in prison and need a second chance. That was why the company existed. The funding came from making and selling clothing such as hoodies and t-shirts.

When I (Michael) hear these things, it makes my soul smile. These high school students have an incredible heart for helping others and a ton of energy to get it done. The nonprofit industry is rapidly growing.

Millennials and Gen Z'ers want to "get their hands dirty" and make a lasting impact within their communities. We call this the work of the church, serving as the hands and feet of Christ.

While we believe nonprofits meet needs in our communities, we do not believe that disciples are being made. Here is the language that we use in our context. If our mission is to make disciples (or however you say that in your context) then food, clothes, money, or other things we provide or do as the church are just the tools we use to build relationships so that we can help them along in their discipleship journey. Simply providing food to a food-insecure person is not accomplishing our mission. Providing food to someone who is food-insecure, building a relationship with that person, and walking with them on their spiritual journey is accomplishing our mission.

We often confuse our mission and substitute meeting tangible needs (transactional) without also addressing the spiritual needs of the person we are serving (relational leading to transformational). We believe that these young people are, in fact, searching for a spiritual connection with others but are confusing the dopamine hit that they are getting from serving "others" with a true spiritual connection with them.

Imagine the church once again providing the opportunity for these young generations to find meaning and purpose in life through a spiritual (faith) community. Imagine these young generations being able to create a gathering at a table in the community with the help of the church to provide a lasting impact.

Asset Mapping

In the work we do with churches through the company we co-founded, Creation Incubator (CreationIncubator. org), one of the first steps conducted with new clients is to take them through a comprehensive asset-mapping process. This process helps churches, nonprofit organizations, and Christian social innovators remove their blinders and see with a fresh set of eyes the full menu of all their resources/assets.

When was the last time your leaders conducted a thorough asset mapping of your congregation? For those who might be unfamiliar with the term, asset mapping provides extensive organizational information about your strengths, assets, and resources. Organizations often limit their inventory of assets to strictly cash, investments, receivables, and real estate. With this limited inventory viewpoint, church leaders are at a great disadvantage in first recognizing the expanded assets of the church. Secondly, the leadership cannot leverage these unknown assets for missional alignment, impact, and effectiveness. Asset mapping gives church leadership a much deeper dive and a more comprehensive understanding of the church's truest and most thorough picture of its assets.

The foollowing is a sampling of our asset-mapping process that helps churches inventory and, thus, leverage all their assets for the best possible Kingdom impact. Our full Asset Mapping Resource leads churches through a comprehensive process to analyze twelve key asset areas.

Asset Mapping: Leveraging Your Real Estate

The investment in the land and facility is often the church's largest asset. Granted, sometimes a church might have a large endowment, but most often, the building and grounds are by far the largest asset owned by the church. As with any asset, the question about being good stewards of such a large asset comes into play. How is this largest asset being leveraged to its fullest potential for the mission of making disciples? This means analyzing the usage of the building for all 168 hours a week, using every square foot of the building, the parking lot, and the property. What are specific ways those hours and that square footage are being used to make disciples, mature disciples into disciple-makers, or create income that is invested back into the ministry to make disciples?

- How much of your building is being used daily?

- How much of your building is being used only a couple of hours a week? How could you imagine leveraging this space more hours per week for missional purposes?

- How much of your parking lot is being used daily? Are there ways to leverage this asset more fully?

- Is there undeveloped real estate that is not being utilized? How can you imagine leveraging this for missional purposes?

Take some time to carefully consider and analyze your building and grounds. We often overlook some assets of the building. For example, some churches have commercial kitchens that are used only a few hours per month. How could you leverage this wonderful asset more fully?

Another thing church leaders often overlook when they analyze building usage is the cost of usage. For example, when daycare or preschools are tenants and pay rent (or not), the cost of utilities, custodial services, wear-and-tear on the building, janitorial and bathroom supplies, and repairs and maintenance to the building and grounds are often overlooked.

One final note: The building should be used for the mission of making disciples or for additional revenue to reinvest in the mission of making disciples. There is no reason to have a tenant in the building that does not serve the mission nor make a profit to benefit the mission.

Asset Mapping: Leveraging FFE

List all your church's major furniture, fixtures, and equipment (FFE) that are not listed in other categories. This would include such items as a portable smoker, office equipment, ceramic kiln, looms, tools, sound boards, mixers, microphones, projectors, screens, speakers, preschool/day school materials, extensive music collection, art collection, noteworthy stained-glass windows, marble baptismal and altar, or any other noteworthy furnishing or fixture.

Asset Mapping: Leveraging Gifts and Experience

One most often overlooked asset area is the congregation's gifts and experiences. This includes secular skills, experience, and training, along with spiritual gifts and passions. Some of these areas include the following: teaching, law, accounting, sewing, art, woodworking, medical, plumbing, electrical, gardening, fishing, hunting, canning, quilting, photography, scrapbooking, sign language, music-vocals and instrumental, interior design, graphics, computer technology, cooking, fitness. Gifts include hospitality, organization, leadership, compassion, relatability, mentorship, networking, time, energy, passion for children/youth/shut-ins, encouragement, mercy, vision, generosity, wisdom, administration, service, etc.

These congregational assets can often be the catalyst for an idea or the gas poured onto a small flame that has needed that certain boost for quite some time. Without this discovery process, neither the voice nor gifts of the congregation will be heard in the process, nor are they likely to be used to bless the community in their need or identified gap.

Asset Mapping: Leveraging Community Partners

Community partners are another important asset to inventory. This asset is an ongoing partnership where more than one person from the congregation is involved. There is congregational involvement, and the asset is usually a prime missional focus of time, energy, commitment, and budget dollars. What person, group, organization, or business does the church already have a relationship with? Name the relationship and how the church and the partner work together. Cite the partnership's purpose, outcome, community impact, and the duration of the relationship. How many from the congregation are involved in the partnership? How many people are involved from the other partner? Repeat this process for each partner relationship.

Again, this is just a small sampling of our comprehensive

Asset Mapping Resource process using twelve unique areas of focus. This foundational step helps discern what kind of Christian social innovation God is calling you to embark upon. Your congregation is blessed with a distinctive set of assets. Having a full picture of your church's assets is critical as you discern how to best leverage these assets for the next faithful steps to launch as a Christian social entrepreneur.

Note: If you are a solo entrepreneur, Creation Incubator will walk you through a similar process.

Identifying Community Gaps

Once your asset mapping is complete, it is now important to identify the community gap your congregation is called to address. Some might refer to this as the problem you will be solving, or your congregational call. Too often, the church sets out to solve a problem or issue that does not need to be solved or one that already has resources and organizations working towards the solution. At this point, the church MUST NOT make any assumptions, guesses, or rely on old information.

How do you find the community gap, community problem that needs to be solved, or opportunity the church needs to take on? You ask. Whom do you ask? You ask the community. Specifically, ask the leaders of your community. Get out in the community.

Note: This is where the work you have done on your emotional and cultural competency will be so very helpful.

Interview community leaders, neighbors, and business owners. Ask questions of community leaders such as librarians, principals, school counselors, nonprofit leaders, social service program leaders, police, firefighters, the mayor, city council members, and the city clerk. Talk with local business owners of all sizes. If your defined mission field involves more than one community (i.e., cooperative parish), repeat this process in all communities.

- What are the greatest needs of the community?

- What community problem/issue/opportunity needs to be solved?

- How could the church help meet those needs, solve the problem, or take advantage of the presenting opportunity?

- What groups are having a positive impact on the community and how are they doing so?

- What groups could use some partners to take their good works to the next level?

- Are there any community projects that need resources, attention, and helping hands?

- What do you know about (name of your church)?

Note of caution and mining deeper: If we are not careful and don't mine for deeper answers, we may not get to the heart of the matter. Too often, we stop when we have identified a transactional need and/or solution. This could be a transactional solution that any charity could address and could be done at arm's length with no interaction whatsoever. While some of this is fine for the church (i.e., providing blankets for the community shelter, providing food for backpacks, providing dollars to buy kids' Christmas gifts), we are searching for relational needs or relational problems needing to be solved. After all, we are the church and in the relationship business. How will we ever have the opportunity to share our faith if we never enter into relationships with new people?

Here is an example of a *transactional* solution:

You are speaking to the school counselor, and she shares that some children come to school with no socks in the wintertime. When asked how the church could help solve the problem, she goes on to share that some donated socks would be wonderful. The church dutifully provides the much needed socks - dropping them off at the counselor's office.

Here is an example of a *relational* solution:

You are speaking to the school counselor, and she shares that some children come to school with no socks in the wintertime. She first suggests the church could help by donating socks, but when asked some more probing questions about why she thought the children came to school with no socks, another solution emerged. The counselor shared that she thought most of the parents of these children were dealing with one of two issues. They were either struggling with how to properly handle their finances (budget), or they were struggling with how to find jobs that adequately supported their families. After extensive conversations, the counselor felt that some budgeting classes for parents (i.e. Financial Peace) and a class on writing resumes, applying for jobs, preparing for interviews, and maybe even dressing for interviews would be extremely helpful. Bingo! There is a relational approach to solving a problem. Invest in people relationally. Walk alongside them; do life with them. Build a relationship with trust and authenticity.

How to uncover a relational solution:

When asking a community leader, business leader, neighbor, or friend about community issues or problems to be solved, listen closely. If the problem and solution are transactional, just keep asking, "What else?" The deeper you mine, you are bound to uncover a golden nugget.

Be sure that you don't hear one suggestion, idea, or need from one conversation and run with it. It is important to have multiple conversations with multiple people to gain a broad sense of the community. You and other leaders of the church are trying to unearth a trend—something that multiple church leaders hear from multiple community conversations. Also, be sure to ask if any other organization is already addressing the identified needs, concerns, or opportunities. If so, is more help still needed, or do you need to identify something else to address in your community?

When talking with people in your community, ask them what they know about your church. It is important to know what the perceptions of your church are in the community. Is the perception accurate? Is the perception current, or is it a leftover perception from a bygone era that has never been transformed? Are the perceptions negative or positive? Remember that it is not for you to confirm or defend their perceptions. You are simply collecting information and educating yourselves.

It is important to approach all conversations with a sense of curiosity, interest, humility, and authenticity. This is a no-judgment zone. Leave your preconceived ideas, assumptions, and traditional church expectations at home. Think of this as a detective adventure trying to paint a crystal-clear picture of the current reality. Stay alert. Notice what is said and not said. Keep thorough notes and identify developing trends in the conversations. Listen way more than you speak.

Multiple church leaders will need to have multiple conversations. One or two conversations will not provide enough information to clearly understand your mission field. Multiple leaders should participate in all these conversations. Dozens of conversations must be conducted and recorded to be analyzed by the entire team later in the process.

Make sure you are having conversations with unchurched people. Since the mission is ultimately to reach the unchurched, it would not be helpful nor provide accurate insights and information to talk only to churched people. If identified, be sure you have conversations with people in the targeted Mosaic. Having conversations with people making assumptions about the targeted Mosaic will likely leave you with false impressions and inaccurate information.

And one final reminder: Be sure you converse with people in your mission field. Again, it's not helpful to gather inaccurate information by talking to people who do not live in the neighborhood/community you are trying to reach.

Spend time walking the neighborhood. Take prayer walks through the neighborhood. Pay attention to what you are seeing, hearing, experiencing, and feeling as you walk. What are you discerning? How is God calling you and the congregation to respond? How does this speak into the vision of God's preferred future for your church?

Ministry AND Income

Once all the demographic data is collected and analyzed, the asset mapping is completed, and the community conversations are conducted, all while praying and discerning, it is time to begin seeing where all of this is beginning to come together.

What needs to be addressed in the community that the church has the assets (including passion and gifts) to do so? At this point in the process, we usually walk possible scenarios through actual business plans and cash-flow projections to see if they are actually viable. Sometimes a dream does not have sustainable cash flow, and we need to be realistic about that fact. Too often, we see churches skip this important step in the process to ensure it is a viable business plan.

Once an idea passes the viability test, it's time to evaluate the steps to launch. Depending on the type of entrepreneurship you are launching, there are a variety of approaches you may want to consider. It may be appropriate to take a big leap and go for it, or you may want to take a different approach and consider what is referred to as a "lean startup" using an MVP (mean viable product) approach. Hiring a coach or consultant with some experience can help you and shorten your learning curve and save you some time, frustration, and dollars.

Let's just name it right here and right now. Christian social innovation can and should be both ministry AND income-generating. There is absolutely no reason it can't be and should not be both. We must get over this pattern of thinking that it has to be one or the other? It can be both.

Just like the church, as a Christian social entrepreneur, it is extremely important to continuously evaluate. Constant evaluation will provide insights and allow you to pivot as needed to stay on track. In addition, you may find your church may not bridge the gap or solve the problem you set out to address. If so, you will then need to adapt and find a different intersection of community need and church assets once again. However, the next time will be so much easier now that the church has become fully immersed into the community!

A church with multiple income streams is likely to be more creative and easier to mobilize when needed, which means the church can ultimately reach more people—the very purpose for which the church exists. Being a mobilized church was the vision in which Wesley launched the church. It was never intended to be a church of people seated on saved pews (aka pew potatoes). No! We were launched as a movement of pioneers doing a new thing to reach new people in new ways. It's time to reclaim our roots and embrace our Wesleyan way of Christian social entrepreneurship that ultimately reached millions of people.

Christian Social Entrepreneurship Examples

Below are examples where both income (profit) and ministry can co-exist:

- Daycare/preschools with intentional ministry integration

- Community gardens with intentional, relationship building opportunities

- Shared workspaces with intentional, relationship building opportunities

- Shared artist spaces with intentional, relationship building opportunities

- Business incubators with intentional, relationship building opportunities

- Food truck ministry with intentional, relationship building opportunities

- Leasing commercial kitchen space for business start-ups

- Counseling centers with support groups as next steps supported by the ministry through leadership and finances as needed

- Thrift stores with intentional, relationship building opportunities

- Coffee shops with intentional, relationship building opportunities

- Housing developments where the church retains presence, care, and ownership

Just imagine how the disciples in a church could bless their community by leveraging the church's assets to meet the community's needs and make a profit that allows even more ministry impact with the community.

Story

In my first church, our preschool was bleeding money and not making disciples. For those reasons, along with several building issues, we decided to close it. This was painful and difficult. Many pastors who have served a church with a preschool have had to make similar decisions. These are not easy decisions but often need to happen for the overall health of the church. Unfortunately, endeavors like preschools within our community can lose their focus and mission and need a "death" so that resurrection can occur.

In the fall of 2016, I offered a sermon on "Dreams." At the end of the sermon, I asked everyone to write down their dreams for this community, and I told them, if they were serious, to put their name on them. Everyone brought their piece of paper up to the front of our worship space and put it in a bowl. We then prayed over these "dreams" at the end of the service. That afternoon, I read each and every single piece of paper. There were things like "start a community coffee shop" and "start a BBQ ministry" on those pieces of paper. We put them in a spreadsheet and glued all of them on a big piece of cardboard. (I still have it in my office today.)

One of the "dreams" was to start an early childhood education facility. It was signed by a young couple in our church. I called them that week and we met at a local restaurant to discuss. They had an existing in-home daycare with seven children in attendance. They thought they would like to expand that into a larger service at our church for the community. The church had four classrooms that were dated and not up to preschool standards. It would be a huge project, but we decided that this was a "dream" we wanted to invest in. We wanted to provide a service to our community by teaching children

Christian principles while also creating revenue for further entrepreneurial endeavors.

So we set off to turn this "dream" into a reality. We remodeled the classrooms. We went through the state approval process. One year later, the dream became a reality. We launched our early childhood education facility in the fall of 2017 with seven children enrolled.

In the next two and a half years, we saw exponential growth. All four classrooms filled up. We had no more space, so we remodeled my office and converted it into a classroom. We moved my desk into a closet. By the end of 2019, we had gone from seven students in two classrooms to eighty students in five classrooms.

Like most preschool facilities, we went from eighty to twenty-seven children almost overnight when COVID-19 hit in March 2020. An estimated 16,000 daycare facilities closed during the pandemic. But through careful management, we were able to get by and remain open. In the fall of 2021, our enrollment skyrocketed, and we surpassed the one-hundred mark. We built two new classrooms and one storage area in our worship space to accommodate this growth.

In May 2022, we purchased a new facility in our community to start a second location to house the "Children's Table" (a learning center - preschool and full-time daycare), ministry, and community space. The Children's Table not only teaches children about the principles of Christianity, but it also provides revenue for other ministries in our community. There is a full ministry integration model within this much needed, revenue-making service provided for the community. Just like any other full-time learning center in our area, we charge market rates for care and treat it like a business, but we also utilize this social entrepreneurship as a meaningful opportunity to make disciples through the Children's Table, our integrated ministry approach at The Table. (See the Conclusion, beginning on page 147, for more information on The Table and The Children's Table).

Evaluator

How open is your church to engaging in social entrepreneurship? Consider the topics below and rate your church on being open to engaging in social entrepreneurship in each topic/area on a scale of zero (not at all open to engaging in social entrepreneurship) to ten (totally open to engaging in social entrepreneurship).

Building

0   1   2   3   4   5   6   7   8   9   10

Land/Outside Space

0   1   2   3   4   5   6   7   8   9   10

Budget/Investments

0   1   2   3   4   5   6   7   8   9   10

Cultural Competence

0   1   2   3   4   5   6   7   8   9   10

Emotional Competence

0   1   2   3   4   5   6   7   8   9   10

Community Engagement

0   1   2   3   4   5   6   7   8   9   10

Community Partners

0   1   2   3   4   5   6   7   8   9   10

Changes in Ministries

0   1   2   3   4   5   6   7   8   9   10

Changes in Focus

0   1   2   3   4   5   6   7   8   9   10

Diversity

0   1   2   3   4   5   6   7   8   9   10

Questions

1. Review the six "success" characteristics identified at the beginning of this chapter. Discuss with other leaders which characteristics your church currently exhibits and which ones your church is currently working towards.

2. Based on your discussion from Question 1, how ready is your church to launch a Christian social entrepreneurship? What brings you and your leaders to this conclusion?

3. What kind of assistance might your leaders need to pursue launching a Christian social innovation?

4. What is your first step if you are considering launching a Christian social innovation?

5. How do you see God working through you and other leaders in your church right now to reach new people in a new way for this new day?

Conclusion

See all of the people?

They are the church.

Without the doors or the steeple!

There is no one way or right way to do ministry. But we know that many of our churches are spending precious time, energy, and resources on ineffective ministries that are not reaching new people. A few years ago, I (Kay) identified an annual conference where about two-thirds of the over eight-hundred congregations reported to have made either no new disciples or only one new disciple in a year. Yes, that's right - more than 500 of over 800 congregations had not made one disciple in a whole year. Unfortunately, this is the rule and not the exception.

As I identified in my book, *Cry from the Pew: A Call to Action for the United Methodist Church,*[43] what other organization would allow this kind of ineffectiveness to continue decade after decade? It is time to call ourselves into accountability and do whatever we must do—whatever it

---

[43] Kay Kotan, *Cry from the Pew: A Call to Action for the United Methodist Church,* Market Square Publishing, 2022.

takes—to become a missionally focused movement once again. Even if it means to evert the church model, turning it inside out.

The purpose of the church has not changed since Jesus commissioned it more than two thousand years ago. But friends, we must be flexible and adaptable in how we offer the Good News for the changing post-modern, post-Christian culture. The mission remains the same, but our methods (how we offer ministry) MUST CHANGE. Most of our methods are broken, and we must figure out how to reach this hurting world in new ways. The days of being upset that the culture has changed and waiting for the culture to change back to church-centric are long past. It is time to move on.

Please join us on this journey to turn your faith community inside out. We invite (and challenge) you to evert your ministry today.

It is time to evert the ministry model!

Evert from Sunday-Centric to
Relationally Focused

Evert from Building-Centric to
Community Minded

Evert from Pastor-Centric to
Laity-Driven

Evert from Offering Plate Dependent to
Multiple Streams of Income where mission is accomplished

It is time to turn ourselves INSIDE OUT!

*From INSIDER-focused to an
OUTSIDE deployed movement*

*From INSIDER-preference-driven to
OUTSIDE focus on the community*

*From INSIDER asset consumption to
OUTSIDE people investment*

*From INSIDER care to
OUTSIDE transformation of the community*

*From INSIDER education to
OUTSIDER focus with the Holy Spirit's
transformation of us and our neighbors*

Please share your stories of turning your church inside out on Facebook at Creation Incubator. If you need help everting your church ministry model, contact us at Info@ CreationIncubator.org to explore a relational, postmodern, post-Christian approach to building faith communities with a unique and innovative approach to ministry.

Michael and Kay have created a working ministry model that incorporates all the best practices offered in this resource built on their combined experience and backgrounds in both the church and secular world. This ministry model is called The Table and is a growing network across the country. The Table is a unique postmodern movement for spiritual communities desiring to reach younger generations through integrated micro communities. The Table includes an exclusive and everted rhythm that is much more appealing to Millennial and Gen Z seekers and new believers. For more information visit CreationIncubator.org/TheTable.

Scott and Kotan also assist churches and church leaders launch other Christian social innovations through their company, Creation Incubators, LLC. One of those Christian social innovations is helping churches launch full time learning centers using an exclusive five-fold system including:

- experiential student education
- social and emotional development
- leadership development
- business/administration development
- ministry integration

In addition, they collaborate with churches and community partners in creating a holistic family approach to family wholeness, health, and well-being through services and programs such as mental health, family services, and concierge services.

Visit **CreationIncubator.org** or send an inquiry to **info@CreationIncubator.org** for more information.

Books By Kay Kotan

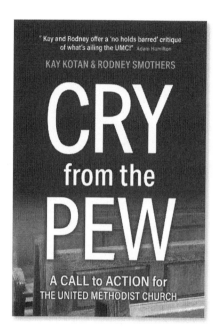

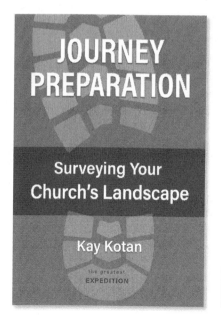

Books By Kay Kotan

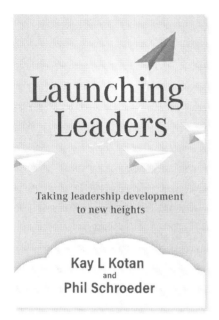

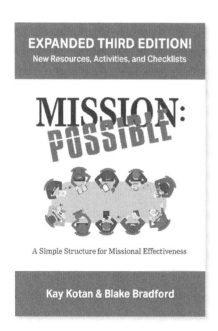

An Effective Approach to Cooperative Parishes

A Congregational Guide to
Discernment and Implementation

Kay L. Kotan & Jason C. Stanley

Foreword by Blake Bradford

Made in the USA
Columbia, SC
19 October 2023

24692501R00100